Everyday Catholicism

Also in this series

Everyday Catholicism:
Seeing God's Action
in Our Lives

Everyday Catholicism:
Real Stories of God
in Our Lives

Everyday Catholicism:
Hearing God's Answers
in Our Lives

Everyday Catholicism

Miracles in Our Lives

LeAnn Thieman, Editor

SOPHIA INSTITUTE PRESS
Manchester, New Hampshire

Sophia Institute Press
Box 5284, Manchester, NH 03108
1-800-888-9344

www.SophiaInstitute.com

Sophia Institute Press® is a registered trademark of Sophia Institute.

ISBN 978-1-64413-163-3

eBook ISBN 978-1-64413-164-0

Library of Congress Control Number: 2020939995

First printing

Contents

2
Angels Among Us

3
Miracles upon Request

4
Everyday Miracles

5
Miracles of Healing

6
Signs from Heaven

Introduction

When my mother was on a spiritual retreat years ago, she posed this question to the pastor: "The Old Testament is filled with stories of miracles performed by God, and Jesus performed dozens more in the New Testament. So why doesn't God still do miracles today?"

The pastor answered, "He does them every day, but we ignore them, dismiss them, or explain them away, with science or as a 'coincidence.'"

After reading nearly 3,000 stories submitted for *Chicken Soup for the Soul: A Book of Miracles*, I suggest there are no "coincidences." While some people recounted miraculous healings and even visions of angels and of God himself, others shared "everyday miracles" that others might have just "explained away."

I've learned that when we "explain away" miracles with science, chemistry, or coincidences, we fail to give credit where credit is due. God may be speaking to us, showing us, blessing us.

I think my grandma had it right. She said that the best proof of a miracle is in the planting of a seed and the beating of a heart.

Indeed, God performs miracles every day. As you read these stories, I hope you'll be alert to identify them in your life. The next time you see a timely rainbow, butterfly, penny, or even a bird, give credit where credit is due.

Look to the heavens, smile, and thank God for His miracles.

—*LeAnn Thieman*

Everyday Catholicism

Chapter 1

Divine "Coincidences"

Well done, good and faithful servant!

—Matthew 25:21

1

Miracle Meeting

Therefore, what God has joined together, let man not separate.

—Matthew 19:6

Growing up with a last name like Miracle made for a lot of puns. When I was born, my parents could honestly say without boasting that I was a Miracle child. On the playground in elementary school I heard, "Hey Miracle Whip!" In junior high school, "It's a Miracle!" echoed through the halls as I carried a toppling stack of books. It wasn't until I reached high school and college that I really found consolation in my name.

I didn't believe I would ever marry, even though that is what I wanted. I would laugh and tell my best friend, "At least I have a good last name because it is never going to change."

Years after my pessimistic marriage prediction, I started my career as a fifth-grade teacher. One day I was walking innocently down the hall, minding my own business after taking my students to the bus. Beth, one of my fellow teachers, emerged from her classroom into the empty hallway.

"There is someone you should meet," she said. Her eyes danced and her lips curled into a smile.

"Oh no," I thought to myself. "Not another blind date." A thousand alarm systems shrilled in my head, and I imagined myself making a U-turn and sprinting, Olympian style, to the nearest exit.

Everyday Catholicism

I was a single newcomer in town and everyone seemed interested in plotting out my love life. As afraid as I was of never getting married, I was becoming more and more afraid of blind dates.

I politely said, "No thanks, I'm already seeing someone," which was true.

Despite my refusal, Beth, without pausing for breath, continued to tell me about Jesse, the nice man she had met at church. Jesse's mother, Sharon, had taught at our school, but died tragically in an automobile accident long before I could ever meet her. Other teachers and past students fondly remembered her kindness, and each year a senior at the high school was awarded a scholarship in her memory. I was sure this devoted woman had raised a nice son; I just didn't like blind dates. Dating in general could be trouble-some, and I certainly didn't want to intentionally invite trouble into my life.

Persistence became Beth's mantra. Each time during the school year when she asked if I would like to meet Jesse, I adamantly refused. I explained that I was dating someone and I was comfort-able with that.

Then that relationship went south, literally.

That summer the man I had been dating left the country on a mission trip, mailing a letter from the airport revealing his decision to end our courtship. Tearing into his letter with great expectation only brought stinging hot humiliation to my cheeks.

It felt like my love life had died a death so dark it was far be-yond resuscitation. My faith told me God was with me, but my doubt made me wonder where He was in my love life. I decided my youthful declarations might be true; it looked like it really would be a miracle if this Miracle ever married.

School started again and I moved to a new apartment. It wasn't my first choice. Plans for another apartment fell through, and by word of mouth, a friend found this one for me near the school.

Those days were filled with definite highs. I loved learning and laughing with my wide-eyed students. When they said, "Miss Miracle, you're the best teacher ever," it softened the hard edges of life. But I was still lonely and wanted to meet someone special—someone with whom I could have a future.

Day after day I graded papers and looked out my new back patio window into the carefully maintained square. A variety of vibrant pots filled with looping vines and late summer flowers clung to neighborly-looking balcony rails. The common area was shared by twelve apartment buildings. I could have lived in any of them. Initially I hadn't considered how choosing this particular building, overlooking this peaceful plot, would be such a good plan for my life.

Months went by. The summer pots disappeared from the square, replaced by snow and ice that clung to the balcony rails instead.

One wintry February morning, I was scraping my car windshield and talking to one of my new neighbors who lived downstairs in my building. He was tall, friendly, my age, and it hadn't taken long for me to notice his movie star smile. When our paths had crossed in the stairwell, we would say hello and engage in brief conversations. If the truth be known, I was developing a crush, and we had never even been formally introduced.

That particular February morning, this handsome neighbor was concerned for the other tenants' safety, as the sidewalks were slick with a thick sheet of ice. He warned each person who walked by of hazardous spots, and I saw how kind he was. We talked as we de-iced our cars, and he asked me where I taught.

"Second Street School," I answered, as my scraper flicked shavings of ice that melted on the warming car hood.

His whole face lit up with interest, igniting his perfect smile. "My mother taught there," he told me with pride.

"Really?" I said enthusiastically. "Would I know her?"

"No." In a quiet voice that sounded far away and tinged with sadness he said, "She died in a car accident."

This tall friendly man began describing his mother's beautiful qualities and telling me about the scholarship that family, students, and friends had started. But his words were muffled, as if making their way down a long tunnel to my brain. My breath caught in the frigid air. My neighbor, who introduced himself as Jesse, was the man I had refused to meet for more than a year. And yet there he was, standing before me.

Much has happened in the nine years since that memorable discovery. My students and I raised money for the Sharon Lewis Scholarship Fund by recycling aluminum cans. My gloomy guess at how life would turn out was wrong. My last name changed after all, and I taught at the school until two days before our handsome baby boy was born.

Now on wintry icy mornings I snuggle close to my husband Jesse in our warm little home and I feel like I'm still a Miracle.

—*Janeen Lewis*

2

Thanksgiving Angel

I do all this for the sake of the gospel,
that I may share in its blessings.

—1 Corinthians 9:23

I was fifteen when my world took a bleak turn for the worst. My mom was diagnosed with cancer … again. The first time had been devastating. She underwent surgery and chemotherapy and she beat the cancer. Then the cancer came back. This time however, there was more to worry about than just the disease my mom was battling. Because of the medical bills she was paying from her previous cancer, this illness left her on the brink of financial ruin. My dad had died years before. It was just Mom trying to hold down the fort. My mom made too much to qualify for any type of assistance and too little to pay the mounting medical bills. I was too young to get a job.

That winter was the worst. We didn't have money to pay for electricity, so we did without. We had a little gas stove that provided heat, and our neighbor let us plug in an extension cord to his home so that we could have one lamp on in our home. The gas stove in the living room was the only heat in the house. I slept on the floor in the living room, as close as I could to the stove without setting myself on fire. Mom slept in her cold room, with as many blankets as we could pile on her.

Everyday Catholicism

Every day and every night my mom prayed and often asked me to pray with her. She thanked God for our blessings, thanked God for each other and always asked God to give us the strength to get through the hard times we were experiencing. She was never bitter, angry, or demanding. She believed God would see us through it. I, on the other hand, wasn't so sure. If God was so good and great, why were we suffering like we were? Why had my mom, who still walked to church every Sunday no matter how cold it was or how sick she felt, gotten cancer again? Sometimes it was hard for me to pray. I was angry at God; I was angry at the world. Life just wasn't fair.

Thanksgiving Day came. I searched our cupboards for food and there wasn't much. I started slamming doors as I looked through the cabinets for a can of food we might have missed. The more I searched the angrier I became. The noise must have woken my mom, because she came to the kitchen wrapped in a blanket. She looked worried for me and she asked, "Baby, what's wrong?"

I retorted, "I'm hungry. That's what's wrong." I wasn't angry at her. I was angry at our situation. I knew I was acting like a jerk, but I couldn't help it.

She opened her arms toward me and said, "Come here. Let's pray."

I rolled my eyes. "Like that ever works." I knew my words had hurt her, but I was too upset to take them back.

She looked at me. The sadness in her eyes killed me. "God hears our prayers. We have a million blessings if you just open your eyes to them. Right now things are hard, but God is here helping us through this. Whatever we need, God will provide. All you have to do is have faith. Pray for what we need and God will answer."

"Oh really, is that so?" I turned on her. "If God is so great, why are we starving? If God is so wonderful, why are we freezing to death in our own house?" The hurt look on her face was more than I could bear. I was sickened by my outburst at her, but I was too angry at God to stop. "Hey God," I yelled up toward the ceiling, "if you are so powerful and almighty, why don't you send us something to eat? In fact, since it's Thanksgiving, why don't you send us a fat, juicy turkey with all the trimmings? Or are we not good enough for you to send us some food?"

I looked at the table scornfully. "Yeah, that's what I thought. I don't see any Thanksgiving dinner. Do you?" I sassed my mom. She stood there, silent tears running down her face.

I was deeply ashamed of what I had done and said, but I was still extremely angry at God and our circumstances. I walked fast, practically running to get out of the house. I yanked the door open, almost colliding with a stocky man in a blue striped shirt carrying an armful of boxes.

"Oh, just in time!" he said and walked in. "Happy Thanksgiving to you both!" he said cheerfully as he put all the boxes on the table. "This big box here is the Thanksgiving turkey, cooked of course. And this one is mashed potatoes; this container has gravy. Oh, and this one here is pumpkin pie, and this one pecan pie...."

Suddenly my ears felt full of cotton. I couldn't hear a word he was saying. I could smell the turkey, the stuffing, all the food in those containers. I could see our little table piled with boxes of food. "So you all have a great Thanksgiving. Now ma'am, if you'll just sign here for the delivery." He handed my mom a pen.

Mom stared down at the paper, but the entire time the deliveryman was staring at me. He had the bluest eyes I'd ever seen.

He took the pen from Mom, thanked her, and as he passed me he touched my shoulder and said, "And God bless you, my child."

I stood there dumbfounded as he walked out of our house and closed the door.

It took a few seconds for me to snap out of it, but I bolted after him. Who was he? Who had sent the Thanksgiving dinner? There had to be an explanation. I ran out to our porch and down the steps, but I slipped and fell because frost covered the steps. I ran to the gate at the end of our cement walkway and out to the sidewalk. There were no cars in sight.

As I turned back towards the house, one thing stood out in the morning sunlight. There was only one set of footprints in the frost that covered our walkway. I stepped closer to the walkway, examining it closely. My footprints were the only footprints that disturbed the frost in our yard.

Whenever God seems far away, I remember that Thanksgiving. I remember the angel God sent to cool my anger. That angel, for I have no doubt that is what he was, showed us that God cared enough to bring us food at our time of need and bring faith back to one girl's heart.

—*Cynthia Bilyk*

A Shower of Roses

But my mouth would encourage you;
comfort from my lips would bring you relief.

—Job 16:5

Excited to see the spectacular fall foliage, my brother Gene flew into New Hampshire from Iowa for a visit. After getting settled, we started out first thing in the morning on the feast of St. Thérèse, October 1, to take in the picturesque beauty of our state. I have a special fondness for St. Thérèse, who promised followers a showering of mystical roses of assistance in times of trouble. As the long day of leaf viewing went on, I grew very weak and tired from my multiple sclerosis. Gene took the car keys, called it a day, and told me to relax as he drove.

We were on a busy highway about an hour from home when a dark sedan sped by us. I heard my brother gasp as I opened my eyes to look out of the front window. With its brake lights still beaming, the speeding car soared into flight, rolling three or four times in the air before landing in the woods.

My brother pulled over to the side of the road and ran toward the overturned car. It was getting dark and hard to see. He yelled back to me, "There is no one in the car." I got my cell phone and called 911.

Everyday Catholicism

Gene walked through the tall grass and woods, constantly retracing his steps, looking for someone. He found car debris everywhere, but no victims.

A few more people stopped by the roadside to assist him. For fifteen minutes they painstakingly searched. Then, in the stillness, Gene heard labored breathing. They found a young man seventy-five feet from the car.

My brother came back to our car. "Diana, I need you. He's still alive. You're a nurse."

I relayed to 911 on the cell phone that the driver had been found. Gene helped me out of the car, down the ditch through the tall weeds, and into the woods. A young man lay motionless before us. Gene helped me sit next to the man's head, took my crutches, and placed them beside the victim's body.

The small man had prolonged gasping respirations and periods of no breaths—symptoms of severe head trauma and near death.

Gene took a flashlight from the car and shone it on the man. He looked barely out of his teens.

I vowed he would not die alone.

I brushed his dark brown hair and looked into his brown eyes that were opened and dull. His neck veins bulged, his pulse was rapid and surprisingly strong.

Then his breathing nearly stopped.

"Take a breath, honey," I said out loud. I grasped his hand in mine. His skin was still warm. I rubbed his cheek and noted the stubby dark growth. "Come on honey, breathe." He took a labored breath.

My back was to the highway, so I was oblivious to the commotion going on. My brother told me that police cars had arrived. Within seconds, I heard a reassuring voice promise that the ambulance was pulling up.

With my face next to the young man's, I talked soothingly, stroked his cheek, and checked his pulse. Still strong. My hair brushed his unblemished face. I couldn't take my eyes off his. "Take a breath, honey." He did. Blood oozed from his mouth and nose. I cleared his airway, stroked his arm, and squeezed his hand in mine. I noticed his blood on my body.

Then silence.

"He's stopped breathing," I called out. His pupils were fixed and dilated. I heard the trooper assure me that the ambulance was here. Paramedics ran down the slope.

As they took over, I kept one finger on the boy's pulse and my other hand grasping his. His pulse grew weaker. His hand cooled.

I prayed, "God if this man cannot be saved, then welcome him with open arms."

When the EMTs positioned him for CPR, the young man's massive head injuries were obvious.

My brother helped me up and brought me to the ambulance. Someone emerged from the back, gowned from head to toe in plastic and rubber gloves, to clean the young man's sticky blood off me. I was shaking. They asked if I needed oxygen, if I was okay. I told them I had MS and always shook. "I'm fine."

It was cold, and we were told to wait in our car and fill out paperwork.

When the state trooper took our report, he said the EMTs had gotten a faint rhythm with CPR. This unknown victim would be transported to the nearest emergency room in critical condition. But it did not look good.

I asked the trooper to tell the boy's family that, once found, he was never alone, that he was never conscious or in pain. That he was prayed for. As a mother, this information would be very important to me.

Everyday Catholicism

Most of the ride home was silent. The entire episode was surreal. My brother alternated between anger and distress because he'd felt so helpless. But there were other feelings, too—a profound love and deep compassion for the boy, someone we didn't even know.

That night the state trooper called to thank my brother and me for calling 911 and for finding and staying with the young man. He had relayed my message to the family just before the boy was pronounced dead.

Gene's last days with us were spent in the White Mountains enjoying spectacular views. There was a peace and quiet understanding between my brother and me. We knew that separately we would have accomplished little at that horrific accident. But together, we assisted a person into his next life. This might have been of comfort to the family. But we would never know.

A year later, October 1, on the feast day of St. Thérèse, I visited my very special Sister in the cloistered monastery of the Precious Blood. She listened intently to our story of the young man and the accident. She sat back, looked at me intently, and said the young man's name.

I was shocked. She had heard this story before.

"Wait here; don't leave," she said.

Within minutes, she brought from the chapel the young man's grandparents who a year ago entrusted St. Thérèse with his care. They'd been seeking the handicapped woman and her brother who didn't leave their grandson's side. Today they were in the chapel to thank St. Thérèse for sending someone with faith to be with him in his time of need.

I imagined mystical rose petals falling softly around us.

—*Diana M. Amadeo*

4

I Will Make Darkness Light

And I will bring the blind by a way that they know not;
I will lead them in paths that they have not known:
I will make darkness light.... These things I will
do unto them, and not forsake them.

—Isaiah 42:16

Even though I am partially sighted and night blind, I knew the bus driver had not let me off in front of the high school for my night class. "Oh no, it's pitch black and I'm lost!" I exclaimed in frustration. "What'll I do now?"

My pulse quickened. Breathing slowly, I tried not to panic.

I prayed while my stomach whirled. "Lord, I've got myself into a mess and I'm scared. You know where I am, and I don't. Please help me find my way."

How could I listen to God's answer while my heart raced with anxiety? I made an effort to calm down.

When I grew quiet, in my turmoil the impression came strongly. "Go to where you can see lights."

I squinted, and where there had been none, I could see a light shining like a beacon in the distance. I felt peaceful. I sensed God guiding me.

As I ventured toward the light, my white cane tapped only cement. Some unseen Power was helping me stay in the middle of the sidewalk.

Everyday Catholicism

I eventually came to what appeared to be a parking lot and found my way to the front of a building. Seconds after going through the doors, a familiar voice called out to me, "Pam, what are you doing here in my church, so far away from your home?"

"Oh, Susan!" I choked out my unbelievable relief to my sister-in-law. "I got lost on my way to a class. The bus dropped me at the wrong stop. I'm so glad to see you!" Then breathlessly, I told her my story.

Susan hugged me. "I just happened to be here for a Bible study at the exact moment you needed to be found. We both know that was no coincidence."

I smiled and nodded my agreement.

While Susan drove me to the high school for my class, I described where I had been walking. As we passed that place, Susan exclaimed, "There are ten-foot-deep trenches on both sides of the path you were on!"

I sat in stunned silence. God had delivered me from imminent danger and led me on paths I did not know.

— *Pam Bostwick*

5

Snapshot from the Other Side

And again, "I will put my trust in him." And again he
says, "Here am I, and the children God has given me."

—Hebrews 2:13

My granddaddy came to see me the night before my mama died. I
was so happy to see him that I gushed like the pump in the yard of
the tenant house where he lived in Georgia when I was a little girl. It
had been years since I had seen my granddaddy, not since his funeral.
"Granddaddy, what a surprise!" I called out to him. "Where
have you been? You must be doing well; you look great!" He looked
rested, relaxed, and young. "I'm so glad to see you. I can't believe
it's you. Is it really you?" I prattled on.

Granddaddy beamed as though he couldn't smile big enough. I
sensed his presence, as if I were standing next to a warm heater on a
cold day. He hugged me close, and I felt sheltered in his loving arms.

"Granddaddy, why are you here? You've been gone so long."

"I wanted to tell you that everything is going to be all right,"
he said.

"Of course it is," I agreed, always the eternal optimist. "Everything's great, even better now that you're here."

He glowed with delight. "It's going to be okay," he soothed.
"Everything's going to be okay." Over and over he assured me
while he petted me like a child. "Everything's going to be all right.

You're strong," he insisted. "You can handle this, and I'll be here with you. You're a strong woman."

I was so happy to see him that I didn't ask what he was talking about. Still smiling blissfully, he said, "We'll all be here with you."

I suddenly realized that my granddaddy was not alone. My grandmother, who died when my mother was seven years old, was with him. My daddy, who had been dead for eleven years, was there. Sick when he died of cancer, he now looked young and healthy. My great-aunt and uncle and other aunts, uncles, cousins, and people familiar and unfamiliar were crowded around. All were joyous and wearing idyllic smiles of eternal blessedness.

As my eyes scanned the relatives who crowded around my granddaddy as though they were having a snapshot made at a family reunion, I saw my mama on the edge of the crowd. I woke up instantly and looked at the clock. It was 2:00 a.m. I felt wonderful, totally wrapped in love and extremely blessed that my granddaddy had paid me a visit. I did not allow myself to question, nor did it register, that everyone in my dream was dead, except my mama.

I later learned that at the same time that my granddaddy came to see me in Murfreesboro, Tennessee, my mama, who lived on an Alabama mountaintop and had no apparent health problems, sat up in bed, turned on the light, and insisted on planning her funeral. Though Ben, her husband, objected and grumbled that he didn't want to talk about it, especially in the middle of the night, she was adamant that he listen to what she wanted done upon her death.

She told him where she wanted to be buried, what she wanted to wear, who she wanted to speak, the songs she wanted sung, and those she wanted notified. She even made him promise to put hay bales around her grave so that her funeral would be like a family reunion and everyone could sit and talk and laugh and visit with one another. She cautioned him not to waste a lot of money on flowers.

When she was sure that Ben understood her wishes, they lay down to sleep.

When my brother Ronnie called later that day to tell me that our mama had dropped dead of a massive heart attack while frying cabbage and making cornbread, I suddenly realized that the dream had been a premonition. "I know," I said, when he shared the shocking news. "Granddaddy was here. He told me."

I knew her spirit had been whisked away for a family portrait to be sent to me in a dream, then returned for a few hours until the exact time of her departure.

I knew why my granddaddy had come, why all my relatives had appeared in my dream, why they were so happy. They were anxiously awaiting the arrival of my mama. They were ecstatically looking forward to seeing her again after many years.

My grandparents were going to be reunited with their baby daughter, my grandmother with the child that she left at a young age, my aunt with a sister that she never met on earth, my daddy with his sweetheart of forty-six years. He had loved her since he first saw her playing paper dolls in a dry creek bed when she was a little girl. My mama's people were gathered to joyfully escort her to her heavenly home and celebrate her homecoming.

My relatives wanted me to know that they loved me, and that they were with me, surrounding me, supporting me. They wanted me to know that everything was going to be all right, that they would comfort and console me in my grief.

To this day I have not lost sight of their loving message. Often I replay the video of my dream and gaze upon the family snapshot that my granddaddy sent to me. It brings me comfort to know that someday we will all be reunited, and I too will be included in the picture from the other side.

—Judy Lee Green

6

The Pretty Lady

Holy Mary, Mother of God, pray for us sinners,
now and at the hour of our death. Amen

—From the Hail Mary

The drone of the HEPA filter and the beeping of the six infusion pumps hooked up to my son's heart almost made me miss his whisper. "Mom. Did you see the pretty lady? Did you see her?"

Cameron had been diagnosed with Acute Myeloblastic Leukemia in June of 1997, one month after graduating high school. Two cord blood transplants and one lung resection later, we were sitting on Ward 9200 at Duke University Hospital. Two days before, the doctors had given me the horrific news that my son was going to die. There was nothing more all the doctors in the world could do, except relieve his pain with morphine.

I had heard that with narcotics some patients have hallucinations. Indeed, Cameron had tried to call his dog Sebastian, who had died the previous year, to his side. Once I caught him eating an imaginary ice cream cone, his tongue flicking out to catch the drips of mint chocolate chip on his arm.

Today seemed different.

I thought Cameron was napping, when he suddenly opened his eyes and began to smooth the crisp white hospital sheets.

The Pretty Lady

Ever vigilant, I had jumped up from the recliner/chair/bed that had been my mainstay, to rush to his side. He kept smoothing the sheets.

"Cameron, is everything alright? Do you need something?"

"She's beautiful. Don't you see her?"

I looked all around the room, but saw nothing.

"See who, Cameron?"

"That lady ... Mary."

"Mary? Your grandmother? Nana?" My mother's name is Mary, and they had always been close, but she was in Wisconsin, as it was my father's turn to visit and stay until the end. "Do you see Nana?"

"No." Cameron was still insistent on smoothing out the sheets, but almost in a patting motion now.

"She said her name is Mary. She said everything is okay. She's beautiful. She's wearing a white dress, and it's really long. It takes up the whole bed."

Cameron kept smoothing the sheets as his face relaxed and he leaned back against the hospital pillows.

"Mom. Did you see the pretty lady? Did you see her?" he whispered.

I nodded my head in affirmation, a pure reflex at this point. Anything to bring Cameron a moment's peace.

I've heard that the Virgin Mary appears to those about to die, and gives them a glimpse of heaven so they will be comforted. I've even heard that she accompanies them on their journey. I'm not Catholic, so I wouldn't know about the traditions and doctrine, but I hope she likes dogs ... and mint chocolate chip ice cream.

—*Dawn Holt*

7

Phil and Louie

Just as the Son of Man did not come to be served, but to serve.

—Matthew 20:28

"Please, Phil, would you look up my son in Vietnam?"

Yup, that was my mom, talking to a complete stranger following a service in our country church in Cottonwood, Minnesota. In one of her letters to me in Vietnam, she told me about the Palermo Brothers, Phil and Louie. They had made five trips to Southeast Asia in the past three years, beginning in 1969, and were headed back there again. Sponsored by World Vision, they were commissioned to minister to military personnel, refugees, prisoners of war, and patients in hospitals, anyone who needed their spirits lifted.

I could just see Mom anxiously waiting for an answer to her question. Didn't she realize there were tens of thousands of Marines in Vietnam?

"Well, ma'am, why don't you write to your son and tell him to look for us? It's possible that we may go to his base," Phil responded. He kept a small book in which he wrote notes from family members in the States to share with sons or daughters in the military. Mom watched as he wrote, "Terry Gniffke, Cottonwood, Minnesota."

Letters from Mom provided more information as she encouraged me. "Be on the lookout for two short Italian guys singing with a guitar and accordion."

I was more than skeptical about connecting with them in Vietnam or anywhere else.

Several months later as I approached the chapel service at Bien Hoa airbase, I thought I heard the sounds of a guitar, an accordion, and people singing gospel music. I was late to the service because the bomb crew and I were assembling bombs and rockets for use by Marine Corps fighter aircraft, providing close air support against the siege of the provincial capital, An Loc.

In the front of the chapel, bouncing along with their instruments, were two short Italian guys singing in familiar Minnesotan dialect. It was just like a piece of home. As a tough eighteen-year-old Marine, I hung out at the back of the chapel, observing the program. Then Phil began talking about a personal relationship with God and how I could have peace in this war-torn place.

Something happened inside my heart and mind as he shared from God's Word.

I could hardly wait to speak to them after the service. When I approached Phil and Louie, I couldn't hold back the tears. "I'm Terry Gniffke from Cottonwood, Minnesota. My mom asked me to look for you over here. She's been praying for years that I would put God first in my life. Would you pray with me?"

That night I committed my life to the Prince of Peace. My mom's prayers for me were answered, and my life transformed forever.

Thirteen years later, far from the war in Vietnam, I was living in southern California, working as an air conditioning salesman. I received a referral to a couple who lived close to my home. When we met, in addition to talking about air conditioning, the three of us began sharing our life stories. The first thing we discovered was that we all had previously lived in Minnesota. When the conversation turned to more serious topics, I began to explain how I had come to faith in God.

"I was a Marine in Vietnam, and one night I went to a chapel service and there were these two little Italian guys...."

Before I could say another word, the woman burst into tears. Sniffling and wiping her eyes, she blurted out, "Those men were my dad and uncle."

Now all three of us were wiping the tears away. The woman, Phyllis, was Phil Palermo's daughter. She and her husband, Jim, had recently moved from Minnesota to California.

A coincidence? No, a divine appointment. A reminder of a mother's persevering prayers for her son so far away from home.

"Where are Phil and Louie Palermo now?" I questioned.

"They were singing evangelists, traveling to fifty-five countries around the world during sixty years of ministry. They worked for Youth for Christ for thirty-seven years and even participated in Billy Graham crusades."

She continued, "Louie and his wife still live in Minnesota, but Dad and Mom live just a few minutes away. I know they'd love to see you again." Phyllis smiled.

Shortly after that appointment, Phil and I met and then had several more opportunities to share what God had done in our lives during subsequent years.

Fast forward eighteen years. At Phil Palermo's memorial service I told our story to hundreds of friends and relatives. I closed with these words: "If it weren't for Phil and Louie Palermo I would not be standing here today, knowing that I will see them again in heaven."

— *Terry Gniffke as told to Darlene Palermo*

8

A Charmed Charm Bracelet

But now, Lord, what do I look for? My hope is in you.

—Psalm 39:7

When I was sixteen, my mom and dad purchased a charm bracelet for me at the very best jewelry store in Syracuse, New York. I was thrilled. The bracelet was fourteen-karat gold and each charm they chose had a significant meaning for me and me alone. There was a golden cheerleader, a small shoe with a tiny diamond in it, and a lovely gold and peridot engraved circle that celebrated my August birthday. I loved that bracelet, and I wore it for every special occasion.

It became even more special to me after Mom died. Even though I was blessed with the world's best father, I missed her terribly, but my charm bracelet made me feel continuously connected to her.

After I graduated from nursing school, I took a job at one of the local hospitals on an orthopedic floor. We were instructed to wear very little jewelry, so the only thing I ever wore was my bracelet; it was on my wrist every single day of my life. It was a part of her, and I felt empty and sad if it wasn't touching me. My patients commented on the beauty of the bracelet, and I was only too happy to tell them the story behind it.

The hospital was located in a hilly area of town, and the nurses' parking lots were at the bottom of the hill. One snowy January morning, I parked my car and started the long trek up to the hospital. I was bundled like an Eskimo in the bitter cold. The wind and snow made the usual climb even more difficult, and by the time I entered the lobby, I was practically frozen. I left my mittens on for a while to warm my hands.

After morning report, I began the narcotic count and readied myself for passing out the day's medications. It was then I noticed that my bracelet was gone!

Devastated, I ran to the locker room and searched frantically for it. I looked in my mittens and hat and shook the scarf silly in hopes the bracelet would appear. But it was nowhere to be found. I felt sick.

I had lost the best memory of my mother.

I could barely concentrate on work, but somehow made it through to the 10:30 morning break. I quickly put my snow gear on and headed down the snowy hill to the parking lot, hoping it had fallen off my wrist and was lying next to my car.

When I got to the gigantic parking lot, I was even more upset. The entire lot had been plowed. Mountains of snow were piled against the fences.

My precious bracelet was lost forever. I walked back to the hospital crying like a child.

One of the nuns, Sister Anne, noticed my tear-stained face and tried to comfort me. I explained my heartbreaking loss. She promised to pray for me, then suggested I say special prayers to St. Anthony, the patron saint of all things lost. I began praying immediately.

By April, I had resigned myself to the fact that the bracelet was gone forever. The original jewelry store was no longer there and no other store in the area carried that special piece. By this time, St. Anthony and I were practically on a first-name basis. Several times a day, I sent him short requests for his intercession in finding my hopelessly lost bracelet. I assumed he was busy with more important services.

One Tuesday morning, another nurse found me in a patient's room.

"The janitor wants to see you."

I was way too busy, so I asked her to tell him I'd connect with him later. I spotted Mike at lunchtime.

He began to explain that this winter had been one of the snowiest ever. The mounds of snow were still melting. I didn't understand what this small talk had to do with me.

"While I was shoveling snow yesterday, I noticed something shiny. For some odd reason, I picked it up and put it in my pocket. Later, I happened to show it to Sister Anne. She suggested I show it to you."

There, dangling from his hand was my bracelet! It was a bit mangled, but it had survived the winter and found its way back to me.

My eyes filled with tears. I could barely whisper, "Thank you," as I hugged him.

The bracelet was repaired to look as good as new. I don't wear it every day now for fear of losing it again, but when I do place it on my wrist, I am very aware of the miracle, thanks to the intercession of my mother and St. Anthony.

—*Marianne LaValle-Vincent*

9

The Heart of a Mother

Hear and let it penetrate into your heart, my dear little
child: let nothing discourage you, nothing depress you.
Let nothing alter your heart or your countenance. Also
do not fear any illness or vexation, anxiety or pain.

—Our Lady of Guadalupe to Juan Diego

In January of 2006 I began praying that my son Ryan and his wife
Jocelyn would have a baby before Christmas of that year. They
had been trying to get pregnant for most of their six-year marriage.

About this time, a friend of mine gave me the prayer that Our
Lady of Guadalupe said to an Aztec named Juan Diego, in 1531, in
Mexico. "Hear and let it penetrate into your heart, my dear little
child: let nothing discourage you, nothing depress you. Let nothing
alter your heart or your countenance. Also do not fear any illness
or vexation, anxiety or pain."

I decided that would be my prayer for the year. I wouldn't let
my heart ache, be discouraged, or depressed, but I would ask Our
Blessed Mother to pray to her son for my children.

The last week of September, my friend who works in a dental
office was working on a patient who mentioned that she worked
for Catholic Charities and that they were really short on couples
wanting to adopt a baby. My friend left the patient and called me
right away. I called Jocelyn at work.

Jocelyn called Catholic Charities the next day and got the information about an orientation that they were having in October. Ryan and Jocelyn attended the classes and filled out the forms to begin the process of adoption. They quickly put together five photo albums with pictures and information about themselves for birth mothers to look at, plus they completed their home study and more forms. On October 31, Ryan took their photo albums to Catholic Charities.

On November 26, I was selling tickets for a church event in the back of the church where several people stood visiting. A young Hispanic man who I had not seen before approached me and motioned me to follow him down the center aisle of the church. He didn't speak English very well but pointed for me to look on the wall where the light was shining up. He asked me in broken English, "Do you see Our Lady of Guadalupe?"

I said, "I'm sorry but I can't."

"I do!" he beamed.

"You are blessed to see her," I simply said.

Four days later, Ryan and Jocelyn came to our house and told us wonderful news. They had gotten a call from Catholic Charities that a sixteen-year-old girl had picked them to be the parents of her baby boy, due on January 28. They were scheduled to meet the birth mother on December 18.

I thanked God that night and told Him January 28, 2007, would work just fine for having a baby for Ryan and Jocelyn.

On December 9, I was sitting in another church with Ryan, waiting for the ceremony to begin. While I was telling him my story of the young Hispanic man, I looked up to see Our Lady of Guadalupe featured on the stained-glass window at the end of our row. I pointed her out to Ryan. During the Mass, the bishop said, "Today is the feast of St. Juan Diego, the man Our Lady of Guadalupe appeared to."

Everyday Catholicism

Ryan and I looked at each other, stunned. He whispered, "Mom, you better go to Mass in three days. December 12 is Our Lady of Guadalupe's feast day."

I seldom go to Mass during the week unless it's Tuesday, when I lead a Bible study. December 12 was on Tuesday.

I went to Mass that day and prayed to Our Lady of Guadalupe all the prayers that were in my heart and thanked our Heavenly Father for hearing my prayers.

At midnight, two days later, the birth mother had an emergency caesarean. The baby was born at 12:45 a.m., weighing four pounds, twelve ounces.

On December 15, Ryan and Jocelyn held their baby, John Paul, for the first time.

On December 23, they brought him home.

There really is no way to describe what I felt as I was at Mass on Christmas Eve. We were there to celebrate the first Christmas gift, a Baby wrapped in swaddling clothes. As I looked at John Paul swaddled in a blanket, my heart was so full of thanks for this most wonderful Christmas gift ... through the intercession of Our Lady of Guadalupe.

—Linda Mainard

10

A Gift to Each Other

Where thou art—that—is Home.

—Emily Dickinson

I was born with a wandering spirit. After college, I joined a theatre company and traveled all over North America and Europe. I was far away and broke most of the time, but no matter where I wandered, I made it home to Colorado for Christmas. This was a fairly significant feat, and yet I had managed to do it every year without fail. It sometimes involved days and nights of driving through blizzards, gallons of espresso, twelve-hour plane rides, lost baggage, and customs officials who always seemed to pick me for scrutiny.

Our holiday traditions were pretty average—tree, presents, way too much food, Christmas Eve service at church, watching the movie *White Christmas* with my sister. Nothing extraordinary happened, but living so far away made it essential to be there. I needed to stay current in my siblings' lives. I wanted to know my nieces and nephews and have them know me. If I wasn't there for Christmas I feared I would just fade out of the family.

My fiancé Calvin and I traveled back to Colorado for our wedding, which was the "opening ceremony" of a huge Fourth of July family reunion. I wasn't a girl who imagined my wedding as the pivotal point of human history anyway, so a simple affair was just my style. But even small and simple broke the bank for us. We headed back to work in Europe knowing there would be a slim chance of another trip home anytime soon. Christmas would likely be a cozy twosome.

"This is okay," I told myself. "We're our own family now. It will be romantic." Plus, our tour ended in Switzerland, so that's where we'd be stuck for Christmas. Definitely worse places to be!

But as the tour drew to a close, my morale crumbled. Watching our teammates excitedly depart, talking about cherubic nieces and nephews, trees, stockings, and family traditions, left me feeling less than lucky about my own situation. Yes, I was a newlywed and the world was supposed to be rosy, but in truth, spending our first six months of marriage in a van with a team of kooky performers and sleeping on pull-out couches in people's dens had placed a strain on the marital bonding process. Our harmony was a little off-key, to put it mildly. Three solid weeks of undiluted togetherness was looking about as awkward as the sixth-grade dance and even less appealing. A little padding of friends and family would have been so much less stressful.

The lack of company wasn't the only check in my negative column, either. We had no home. Like I said, we traveled in a van and were housed as part of our performance contracts. Being on break meant that we'd have to find a place to stay. Someplace free. And who wants a couple of bickering vagabonds hanging around at Christmas? Even if someone did take pity and invite us into their "stable," I was really stretching to dig up any gratitude for someone's pull-out couch.

Then there was the shortage of trappings and trimmings. Our performing-artist-lifestyle left us without discretionary funds, so gifts were pretty much out. And to top it all off, Calvin got sick with an infected wisdom tooth. He was delirious with pain. So much for romance.

First things first. Although Calvin and I were alternately ticked off and bewildered by one another, I did still have regular moments of fondness toward him. I didn't enjoy seeing him in pain. Especially because it made him all whiny and meant I had to do all the driving. We needed to get that tooth taken care of. We prayed.

"Lord, we haven't been very nice to each other lately and we know that bothers You. We're going to try and improve, but in the meantime Calvin's in a lot of pain and it's Christmas and all, and we were hoping that maybe You could toss us a miracle or something. A little sprinkle of healing power. Please."

It was something like that. Not a very spiritual-sounding prayer, just desperate. We stopped on our way out of town at the home of our area representative, Jean-François, to drop off a calendar for our next tour.

He took one look at Calvin and declared with widened eyes "zut alors!" This can mean many things, but in this case it was an expression of alarm.

He made a phone call. He spoke way too fast for me to follow his French, but it sounded very emphatic and convincing, and twenty minutes later the source of distress was being extracted from Calvin's jaw by Jean-François' friend, who also happened to be a dental surgeon and who also decided he didn't want to be paid since it was two days before Christmas. God is so cool, and His people can be really cool sometimes too. On this day He was also really speedy, which was such a nice bonus.

While Calvin was being repaired, I wandered the streets of Lausanne soaking up Christmas Spirit from all the colors and lights and using my tiny store of Swiss francs to buy a few chocolate coins, a nice writing pen, a recording of Calvin's favorite artist, and a few other tidbits. I could wrap each one separately and tie little bows and we could have a miniature Christmas. It would be a peace offering—my promise of a fresh start. Our harmony had already improved with the pressure of touring off our shoulders. A little privacy might be tolerable after all.

Everyday Catholicism

With that thought came the reminder that we needed a place to stay. We actually had an offer, but I had put off phoning them. Timothy and Pierette were the elderly uncle and aunt of a colleague. They lived in a remote mountain village a couple of hours from Geneva, and we had met them earlier that tour. Timothy was an egg farmer and Pierette ran the general store in the village. They mentioned that they had a little apartment in their basement and that we were welcome to stay anytime, including the holidays.

Why hadn't I called them? I had a picture in my mind of a spider-infested stairway leading to a dank room with a bare flashlight hanging down, a chamber pot in one corner and a hot plate with questionable wiring in the other. I was thinking WWII, French Resistance. This would be the space between two walls where they hid Jewish neighbors and secret radios. Of course this was neutral Switzerland, so none of that actually happened here, but my imagination always tended toward the dramatic. There would be an old wooden door with a broken latch. Chickens would be pecking outside the door and snow would blow in through the cracks. We'd sleep on separate army cots under threadbare blankets and we'd have scrambled eggs for Christmas dinner. Truthfully, I was kind of reveling in the whole sad and wretched picture and imagining the screenplay.

I was brought back to reality when Calvin arrived, all swollen-cheeked. "Tho, dith joo make dath phwone cawwl?"

Darn. We really had no alternatives, but I was sure the experience itself wouldn't be as fun or glamorous as the eventual movie version. I prayed again. "God, I miss my family. So far, marriage is not really what I expected, and I feel like Heidi going to stay on some mountainside in a scary basement with some old people I don't really know. I want to make the best of this. I know it's really not all about me. I know I should ask You to help me grow up and be selfless like You, but I also want to pray that we have a really nice, fun holiday together."

I made the call, got directions, and turned the van up the winding mountain road. As we pulled into the little town, we had to wait for a herd of cows making its way down the main street. With Calvin mumbling the directions through wads of cotton, we arrived at Pierette's general store.

I knocked hesitantly. The door flew open and Timothy and Pierette greeted us like their own grandchildren back from a war, or a refugee camp, or from just having received a Nobel Prize. We were ushered directly into the parlor where a fire was crackling and a tree was twinkling. There were cookies right out of the oven, and hot chocolate with lots of whipped cream.

Over steaming cups they asked us all about our tour, all about our wedding, all about our families. We learned all about egg farming and life in a tiny Swiss village. We laughed and smiled and ate cookies. God had answered our prayer. He knew what our marriage needed, and He prepared this place for us long in advance. This was the most calm, nurturing place in the world to spend Christmas, or any other day for that matter. Of course I hadn't seen the little apartment in the basement yet, but Pierette said we were welcome to join them upstairs as much as we liked, so maybe we wouldn't have to hang out with the spiders.

The phone rang, disrupting our relaxed conversation. We heard a "zut alors!" in the conversation. Timothy returned to us with a frown.

The village was in an uproar. The pastor was sick. He had a fever and had lost his voice. There would be no Christmas Eve program. This was a considerable crisis, tantamount to the plague or a foreign army marching over the Alps. Timothy and Pierette exchanged distressed glances and Pierette immediately began clearing away the dishes. Whenever a solution is unclear, it's always helpful to tidy up in Switzerland.

Calvin raised an eyebrow at me, and I answered with a grin and a nod. This was a no-brainer! We jumped up and offered to save the day.

We'd been doing nothing but Christmas programs for weeks. We had a vast repertoire to choose from. Relief spread over our hosts' faces.

We began gathering props, running lines, and planning all the music we could do with only the two of us. With a quick change of clothes we set off. We chose a play about two lonely people who meet in an airport on Christmas Eve. As the characters hesitantly begin to converse, they share their stories, their loneliness, and a reminder of God's gift to us in the birth of Jesus. My character, a believer, realizes that they were put there for that reason—put there to answer one another's need. They read the Christmas story from the book of Matthew, and share an impromptu celebration.

Calvin's character, with spiritual eyes opening for the first time, declares, "You'll have to lead me. I've never had a real Christmas before."

We were in the zone. We were a perfect team that night, and I remembered why I had chosen to spend the rest of my life with this man. Performing this play on Christmas Eve, for these people, was perfect. As I spoke my lines, the truth of them penetrated my own heart—we answered each other's need. We were put here for that reason. The paradox of God's sovereignty struck me. Somehow, in the complexity of God's love and provision, He cares about my smallest details and desires. And yet, at the same time, it's all about Calvin, and it's all about the man in the front row with tears streaming down his cheeks, and it's about Pierette and her general store, and the dental surgeon, and all of my teammates at home with their families. We are God's gift to each other. Like a master composer, He brings all the instruments together, each with a different tone, each playing a different part, and He makes it turn out so beautifully.

After the program we were invited to the evening meal, full of cheese and chocolate and all the yummiest Swiss things. Not a single scrambled egg. Later, we grabbed our suitcases and at last made it down the staircase to the place that would be home for the next three weeks.

The staircase was steep, and the basement was indeed dark and creepy. We opened the apartment door and were greeted by twinkling lights, a small decorated tree in the corner, and evergreen boughs, all adorning a newly remodeled, sparkling clean studio. There was modern plumbing and a kitchenette with perfect wiring. There was a tantalizing fruit basket on the table and a big, soft bed covered with the whitest and fluffiest down comforter I'd ever seen. Calvin spontaneously lifted me over the threshold.

"Merry Christmas," I sighed. He set me down, wrapping his arms around me. I wrapped back. We were God's gift to each other.

—*Kristi Hemingway*

11

Christmas Grace

*You are the most excellent of men and your lips have been
anointed with grace, since God has blessed you forever.*

—Psalm 45:2

Snow continued its determined onslaught outside the assisted living facility windows. By late evening, I grew anxious about how the roads would be when I headed home. It was the week before Christmas. I should have been on my way home by now. The evening receptionist who was scheduled to relieve me had phoned to say she'd been unable to get her car started. Why was I the unlucky one stuck behind a receptionist's desk when I should have been home sipping hot cocoa and decorating the Christmas tree?

The telephone shrilled. Answering a little grouchily, I heard a man's voice. "Is this Avis rental car?"

I tried to remain calm. "No, I'm afraid our phone number here at the assisted living facility is one digit different than Avis. Let me give you that number so you don't have to look it up again." Sighing, I quickly glanced at the familiar number of the car rental company on the pad of paper in front of me. I finished giving the gentleman the number, wishing him a Merry Christmas. Just as I was about to hang up, I heard his voice in midair.

"Wait a minute please!"

"Yes?"

"I know this must sound insane, but I have to ask: do you believe in miracles?"

I sat straighter in my chair, startled at such a question from a total stranger.

"Definitely; why do you ask?"

"I'll try to make a long story short. My parents recently passed away in a car accident. I have no one left in the world but a grandmother somewhere in Virginia who I haven't seen since I was little. An uncle placed my grandmother in an assisted living facility when he grew too ill to care for her any longer. He's gone on to heaven as well. I have to ask: Do you happen to have a Grace Sheperd at your facility?"

My heart beat faster as I recognized the familiar name. I pictured the gentleman holding his breath on the other end while I listened to the pinging sound of the icy precipitation pelting the window to my right.

"Are you still there?" he asked finally.

"Yes, I'm here. I wish I could give you the information you're after. I'm afraid there's a privacy policy that prohibits me from answering. The director of the facility will be in her office on Monday morning, however."

"I understand your responsibility in protecting the residents." The young man sounded so sad. "Thank you for your time, and Merry Christmas!"

"Wait!"

"Yes?"

"Virginia is a beautiful state to visit at Christmas time! Let me give you our address in case you happen to be traveling through our area any time soon!"

"Bless you!"

Christmas Eve I arrived at work earlier than usual. Christmas lights twinkled on the decorated trees up and down the hallways.

Carols drifted from beneath a resident's closed door as I delivered the morning papers.

I was passing Grace Sheperd's room when I suddenly froze in place. Grace sat in her usual rocking chair, her Bible open in her lap. Seated on the stool directly in front of her was a handsome young man with curly dark hair. His hand gently clasped Grace's as she read *The Christmas Story*.

Suddenly Grace spotted me. "Paul, here's the woman who helped you find me! Mary, please come and meet my grandson, Paul!"

I hurried inside as tears clouded my vision. The young man slowly rose to his feet, taking my hands in his.

"How can I ever thank you for leading me to my grandmother?" Shaking my head, I attempted to talk around the enormous lump in my throat.

"We both know it was a Christmas miracle!"

"Yes it was … Merry Christmas!"

"Merry Christmas, Paul. Merry Christmas, Grace!"

Making my way back to the reception area, I sent a silent prayer heavenward.

"Father, now I know why I was meant to stay late the other night. Thank you for the miracle of Christmas and for your abiding grace … Paul's Grace too!"

I couldn't help smiling. It was going to be a glorious Christmas!

—*Mary Z. Smith*

12

Family Resemblance

Trust in the Lord with all your heart,
and lean not on your own understanding.

—Proverbs 3:5

Mrs. Martina Himes, a woman I'd never met before, took one look at me and uttered seven words that changed my life forever. Not more than ten minutes after I arrived at my girlfriend's party, she gave me the once-over and then announced, "Girl, you look just like Sandra Penn!"

I'd been searching for my birthmother for more than twenty years. All I ever knew about her was that her last name was Penn. After a brief conversation with this enchanting woman, I knew in my heart that this was no coincidence. Mrs. Himes began to cry as we agreed that God had brought us together for something awesome. We could feel it.

Although she'd spent most of her adolescent years hanging out with this Sandra Penn, she hadn't laid eyes on her in fifteen years. She hadn't even thought that much about her, until now.

Our search for Sandra Penn began. Mrs. Himes's sister was the one who'd last been in touch with her. All she had to do was find Sandra's phone number and call her.

Two weeks later, she did. And that was it. Seventeen days after meeting Mrs. Himes, my lifelong needle-in-a-haystack search for my birthmother was over, because the "needle" called me on my cell phone.

We were reunited two Saturdays later, exactly one week after my thirty-fourth birthday. The minute I laid eyes on Sandra, my birthmother, I understood what all of Mrs. Himes's fuss was about. I really did look just like her. I'd been obsessed with family resemblance ever since I could remember. For all of the wonderful gifts that Mom and Dad (my adoptive parents) gave to me, resemblance was not among them. I didn't have Daddy's eyes or Momma's smile or any other unique physical trait that belonged to them. When my birth family came rushing through my door all at once that day — my mother, my brother, my sister, and my little niece — there was family resemblance as far as the eye could see! Not only do I look like my mother, I'm the spitting image of my younger sister too. My brother looks like a combination of us all and my niece looks like my sister and like me.

God had, indeed, brought us together for something awesome. We could feel it.

—Pam Durant Aubry

Chapter 2

Angels Among Us

*In the visions I saw while lying in my bed,
I looked, and there before me was a messenger,
a holy one, coming down from heaven.*

—Daniel 4:13

13

Angel in the River

*An angel from heaven appeared to him
and strengthened him.*

—Luke 22:43

My younger sister and I were on a summer vacation with our aunt and uncle. At the time I was still a non-swimmer, and naïve to the dangers of the river. As my uncle and aunt relaxed on the beach with my sister and cousin, I could hardly wait to jump in the cool water. They cautioned me to stay close to shore.

I didn't have flotation devices, and I was unaware that I was slowly creeping away from the beach. All of a sudden I couldn't touch the sandy bottom with my feet. How did I get to the middle of the river? Afraid of getting in trouble for disobeying the rule, and jeopardizing any future camping trips if I survived, I didn't yell out for help. Sounds silly, but I was only seven and cursed with being too shy.

Within seconds I had already gone under twice, gasping, and running out of air. The far-off voices of others in the water and on the beach were now muffled. Just as I was going down a third time, out of nowhere appeared a handsome smiling man with blond hair. He was within inches of me and had hauntingly beautiful blue eyes. Neither of us spoke a word. With his index finger to his lips, I knew he was assuring me this was our secret about me drowning. Strange as that sounds, I was relieved no one would know. In my mind I distinctly heard, "Everything will be okay." No one was near us, and the man never reached out to touch me.

Within a flash I was back at the shore! The moment my feet touched the sand, I could clearly hear the voices of everyone in the distance. My uncle and aunt were still at the same spot on the beach, unaware of the near-tragedy that just transpired. I quickly glanced back at the river, searching for the blue-eyed stranger. He was gone! I couldn't comprehend what had happened. Only a few seconds had passed, and I was no longer in the middle of the river drowning. How could I be back safely on shore without feeling myself move, and why did the mysterious man vanish? I wanted to say thank you.

I kept my secret for forty years before I figured out the blue-eyed man was my guardian angel. I was almost fifty when I finally shared my river experience with Mom. She was naturally upset that I hadn't yelled out for help—and amazed I could keep this secret for so many years.

As a child I had no way of understanding what happened at the river. Over the years though, I've experienced many other close calls, some even life-threatening, with outcomes that didn't always make sense. I knew I wasn't alone. God always sent my angel in the nick of time. He never appeared again as he did in the river, but I felt his presence and heard the voice in my head, "Everything will be okay."

My favorite childhood prayer, long before I met my angel at the river, was to my guardian angel. Even now, as a grandmother, I always end my prayer time with "Angel of God, my guardian dear, to whom God's love commits me here. Ever this day, be at my side, to light and guard, to rule and guide. Amen."

—*Connie Milardovich Vagg*

14

The Boy

And the prayer of the faith will save the sick person,
and the Lord will raise him up.

—James 5:15

A young boy lay in the critical care ward of Children's Hospital in Denver. He was thin and weak from years of struggling with uncontrolled asthma and chronic bronchitis. Even though he had been wasting away for years, he had never quit fighting for every breath. Now a severe case of pneumonia was taking away what little strength he had left. He lay in his oxygen tent listening to the muffled voices of those who came to visit him. He'd joke with his parents and tell them the worst part of being in the plastic enclosure was that it made the toast soggy, but he could see even through the foggy plastic that it was taking its toll on them, too. As he got sicker, he joked less, sat up less, and heard less of what was going on around him.

One morning, as his parents sat by his bedside, the boy's doctor came in and whispered something to them. What the young boy couldn't hear was that the hospital staff had done everything they could, but the pneumonia was winning. The doctor suggested they call a priest. Soon a man in clerical dress was standing next to the boy's bed. He pulled up the side flap of the tent and, praying, he anointed the child with oil.

Everyday Catholicism

The rest of the day passed in a flurry of activity that seemed to happen in silence. Things in the hospital changed. The staff rotated and new patients came, while the well patients were released. The one constant seemed to be the boy in the tent and his mother sitting by his side, waiting.

His mother was a woman of faith. As she waited for the inevitable, she prayed, silently, so she didn't disturb her son. She prayed late into the night until she had said to God all she could say. And then, she waited some more, with only the sound of the machinery to keep her company.

The boy was waiting too. He waited to catch his breath. He waited for the pressure in his chest to go away. He waited for the struggle to end. He waited in silence. He was waiting and listening to the silence when he heard her voice. She said, "Don't worry. Everything's going to be alright."

He opened his eyes. The flap of the oxygen tent was still down. Funny, she had sounded so clear, like she was right next to his ear. He turned toward his mother and said, "Mom, you sounded just like an angel when you said that."

His mother looked up. "Said what?"

I think of this story whenever I feel alone. In today's world, sometimes it feels like the more people we have around us, the more electronic gadgets we have to help us communicate with each other, the more isolated we feel.

As Catholics we've got to remember that grace from our Father fills us, that intercession from the saints and our Holy Mother is only a prayer away, and that we are under the constant watch of the angels.

I know that for a fact. You see, I was the little boy.

—*Jeffrey Brooks Smith*

15

Angel Guide

Last night an angel of the God whose I am
and whom I serve stood beside me.

—Acts 27:23

In the middle of a Vermont mud season, my husband, two young children, and I welcomed my father into our home. He was hoping for a full recovery from pneumonia so he could go back to retirement and his cabin on the coast of Maine. The pneumonia was brought on by the chemotherapy that wracked his old body.

One evening, while folding laundry in the living room, piling little pairs of tights next to tiny T-shirts with trucks and tractors on them, my dad sat on the couch and watched. The top of his bald head was slightly fuzzy, his stomach was bloated and his cheeks sunken. "You know," he said, like he had just remembered something funny, "there's something we've all been forgetting about."

"What's that, Dad?"

"The cancer!" he said.

Maybe he'd forgotten about the cancer, but no one else had. He had a type of liver cancer for which there was no cure, and because of the pneumonia, he was not able to finish the trial treatment he'd been receiving. Not that it was helping anyway. Everyone but him knew the end was slowly drawing near.

Everyday Catholicism

One night while my husband was out grocery shopping and I was putting the kids to bed, my father called to me from downstairs. I could tell by his strained voice that something was wrong. Running down, the children close behind, I found him on the couch. He was breathing like he had just run a marathon. His face was red and his eyes were wide with pain. Even while calling 911, I realized he was not to have a slow cancer decline after all. This heart attack would bring a quick end. "Go in the living room and watch for the ambulance," I told the children, surprised at how calm my voice sounded. I didn't feel calm inside; it felt like a tornado was ripping me apart.

My heart pounded so loudly that I could hardly hear the medic on the phone give me directions for CPR. "I can't do this," I thought, yet I tipped my father's head back, pinched his nose closed, breathed into his mouth and pumped his chest. "This isn't really happening; it's just a bad dream, and where is that ambulance anyway?" The road we lived on was muddy and long; it would be a while until they arrived.

I knew he was dying, but I also knew that for some reason I had to continue keeping him alive. I held my mouth against his, wishing it didn't remind me of a kiss, wishing his breath didn't smell like the chicken soup we'd had for supper. Wishing this wasn't happening. Once while pumping his chest I felt something crack. "I think I broke a rib!" I said to the stranger on the phone. "That's okay," he said. "It happens." I breathed and pumped and was glad the children were spared this strange and horrifying sight. "Don't forget to tell me when the ambulance arrives," I called to them. And please, God, make it soon.

When they did finally arrive, they had machines to do the CPR. A young medic wearing a Red Sox cap looked at me kindly and said, "We'll do all we can, but it doesn't look good." I knew that and never doubted that this was about his death. They also told me I had done a great job; my efforts had saved his life. Whatever that meant at this point.

My husband met me in the emergency room. We watched as my father's breathing slowed. I didn't want him to go. I wanted to cry out, "Come back," but his body lay like a statue on the table, his blue eyes stuck open, seeing nothing. The short gasps of breath were slowing down. It was his time, but I didn't want it to be. I wanted him to get better and go back to his house on the coast where we would visit him and eat lobsters and mussels, watch the sun rise out of the sea, play Scrabble and backgammon, where he would read his mysteries and walk the beaches, content and happy with his sweet life. I wanted him to watch my children change from little to grown, to guide me through all that was still to come.

Even though I was standing right next to him, I felt far away, dizzy and unbalanced, like I was on a ship in a storm. Surrounding the bright hospital lights I saw black dots everywhere and I wondered if I might pass out. Still, I tried to comfort him. "He needs help," I thought. "Should I say something like 'it's okay to go'? But I don't want him to leave!"

Watching over him, I became aware of someone standing directly behind me. Strangely, I didn't need to turn around to be able to see her clearly. She was like an angel, a little taller than I, dressed in flowing, golden silk. Her black hair fell around her glowing face, and her eyes told me I had nothing to worry about. Ever. She was the most calm, yet powerful, force I had ever known. Although she looked like she was made of light, I found myself leaning into her arms. She held me so completely it felt like I had merged into her. I did not have to hold myself up anymore. As my dad took his last breath, and as I was held by this angel, I raised my arms up and up and up, guiding his spirit with my hands toward heaven.

Late that night, I sat alone at my altar. In front of God I cried for my dad, for me, for the intense feeling of loss. Feeling a sudden need to sit quietly, I became aware of a voice speaking to me. I could feel that it was the angel from the hospital, so I steadied my breathing and listened. "Your father came to you for his death," she said, "to learn about God. You breathed God into him as he was dying." My father had been a strict atheist.

The next day, recounting the sacred experience of watching my father die, I told someone about how I raised my arms up and up, guiding his spirit. My husband, present for this conversation, said, "No, you had one hand on his chest, and the other on your own. Don't you remember?" It sounded familiar, and I remembered my hands in that position, a hand on both our hearts, and feeling the energy pour through me to him, his chest rising for the last time. "Yes," I said, "I do remember that, but I also remember seeing my hands guiding him up. How can that be?"

And then I remembered the angel who held me, and knew it was her hands, reaching around me, lifting my dad to heaven.

—*Lava Mueller*

16

The Angel

Do not forget to entertain strangers, for by doing so some people have entertained angels without knowing it.

—Hebrews 13:2

I closed my eyes and daydreamed in the cramped seat of the airplane. While the jet carried us across the Atlantic Ocean, my thoughts went back to when I was four years old living in a tiny English village.

I had admired my brother, Sonny, a handsome sailor in the British Navy away at war in WWII. After the war, he served in Hong Kong, his favorite place in the world, and I lovingly learned to write HONG KONG — the first words I ever wrote — on the envelopes to him.

Over the years, the relationship with Sonny and his family and our parents became strained. I only saw him a couple of times over a period of twenty years. I moved to the U.S., but I visited my hometown in England every year that I could. This trip, my cousins and I chatted as we drove around the cool and windy sea air in the county of Norfolk.

"Sonny is buried somewhere around here," I piped up at one point.

"Don't you know where his grave is?" cousin Brenda asked.

"No. As you know, Mum died earlier in the same year and no one else had contact with him."

"Sad how families drift apart."

"I remember the hospital's name. It's near Cromer, so I suppose he'd be buried near their location," I said.

We spontaneously decided to find his grave. So the day proceeded. We checked with the city's registry office. No James Arthur Goodwin, Sonny's real name.

The wind whipped around us as Brenda, her husband, Tony, and I methodically read every gravestone in several small cemeteries. No luck.

We drove past thatched cottages and country gardens. "Here's a nice large graveyard," Brenda said, pointing at a black and white sign. Tony drove through the entrance and parked the car in the graveled parking area.

We began our search in a cold drizzle, walking forlornly up and down the neat rows of gravestones and monuments. A caretaker with blond hair rode by us on a small tractor. He stopped, turned off the engine, and watched us. "Can I help you?" he asked. He removed his work gloves and placed them on the tractor seat.

"I'm looking for my brother's grave," I offered. "He was nearby in hospital when he died."

The caretaker smiled at me. "I just happen to have the key to the chapel over there." He pointed to a building across the parking lot. "All burials are recorded there. If you know about when your brother died, I can look in the record book to see if he's resting here."

"Yes, I know it was in January 1982," I said, breathless, as we tried to keep up with him. The caretaker stuck a large key in the door lock. It turned with a thunk, and the door slowly opened.

Inside, on a shelf covered in dust and dead flies, was a large ledger book. The caretaker blew off the dust and opened it to 1982. He ran his finger down the columns of names. "Yes, here he is—James A. Goodwin. Grave number 136."

"I'm so relieved," I said quietly. "I've found him at last." My cousins nodded in agreement.

We followed the caretaker out to the grave numbered 136. We stared at the unkempt rectangle. "It's unmarked," I gasped. "I can't believe his family left him in an unmarked grave." A sob caught in my throat. My brother had been dumped here, alone, with no marker. Not even a vase of fake flowers.

We thanked the caretaker, and he drove his tractor to the back of the church.

Brenda wiped away a tear. "Why don't we find a monument maker and have something made with his name on it?"

"Just what I was thinking," I said. "I only have a couple of days left on vacation so we have to do that soon."

"We can go to one on the way to our house," Tony piped up.

After many wrong turns through Cromer's streets, we found a monument maker. I chose a marble vase engraved with Sonny's name. It would be ready for delivery to the cemetery in a few months.

I returned to the U.S., where my life plodded on uneventfully.

Then Brenda called me one afternoon. "We just got back from Cromer," she told me.

"Did you go to the cemetery?"

"Yes, but listen to this." She paused. "We were walking toward Sonny's grave, and there—wait for it—the same caretaker was at that moment taking the marble vase out of his car."

"No. I'm astonished," I burst out.

"Unbelievable," Brenda said. "We followed him as he walked to Sonny's grave and gently placed the vase in the soft ground."

"Did he say anything?"

"He quietly said, 'Just a coincidence.' Then he walked back to his car and drove off." Tony added.

"We wanted to thank him, so I called the church to see how I could contact him," Brenda continued.

Everyday Catholicism

"And did they give you his phone number?"

"They said they didn't have a blond caretaker. The man who's cut the grass for the last twenty years has dark skin and black hair."

We fell silent. My skin crept with goose bumps. I suddenly remembered that I had never told the blond caretaker my brother's name, just the month and year of his death, when he had looked up his gravesite in that dusty ledger.

"I think we've met an angel," I said.

"We think so too," Brenda whispered.

"Amazing. He found Sonny for us."

"Amen."

—Rosemary Goodwin

17

My Brother's Keeper

And your children I will save.

—Isaiah 49:25

It happened almost twenty-five years ago, when my brother was three and I was six. We were spending the day at my grandmother's house and I snuck off to her bedroom to play. My brother, Ryan, who followed me everywhere, came along. I didn't need to explore long to find what I was looking for. The small bottle of red nail polish lay in plain sight on the dusty oak dresser.

I sat on the floor in the open doorway and painted my nails. As usual, it was a messy job and by the time I was halfway through, the thick smell of nail polish surrounded me. I had been warned not to do this on several occasions, so every few seconds I looked down the hallway to make sure my grandmother wasn't coming.

Behind me, Ryan amused himself by using the old-fashioned bed spring as a trampoline. "Creak! Creak!" it loudly complained under his assault.

Just as I was finishing my nails, I felt a light tapping on my shoulder.

Ryan and I were alone in the room so I spun around expecting to find him.

Strangely though, he wasn't there.

"Where are you?" I asked into the empty space.

Everyday Catholicism

Thinking he had ducked under the bed, I pulled the sheet back and got down on my knees prepared to yell out, "I found you!" But I was stunned when I didn't find him there.

I grew worried and quickly began opening closet doors, frantically searching for my little brother. I'd been sitting in the doorway the entire time so I was certain he had not left the room.

As I got ready to open the last closet door, I felt the tapping on my shoulder again, more urgent this time. I spun around for the second time … and saw my brother's legs hanging over the second-floor bedroom windowsill!

My heart raced. I ran to him, overwhelmed by fear that I would not reach him in time.

But I did. Holding on to him and pulling backwards with a strength I am still surprised I possessed at age six, I hauled him back safely into the room. We landed with a loud thud on the floor, breathing heavily.

I was so relieved, we just sat there hugging tight for a long time.

Me, my brother, and his guardian angel.

—*Romona Olton*

18

Rain Man

The golden moments in the stream of life rush past us
and we see nothing but sand; the angels come to visit us,
and we only know them when they are gone.

—George Eliot

It had been raining hard off and on for a few days, and in San Antonio, Texas, as much as we usually need rain, that much is dangerous. Roads flood quickly, and the number of high water rescues, injuries, and deaths go up.

My mother-in-law Marlene had invited us for dinner at her house, and we'd been there for much of the day. Three of our five children were with us: Ryan, our teenager, plus our two little girls, Alana and Rachel. Our other two daughters were spending the night with friends.

As we headed home to the other side of town just as darkness began to settle in, the rain had dissipated somewhat. It gradually began to increase, however, the closer we got to downtown.

"Alan, maybe we should take the 281 instead of going through downtown," I said, thinking that accidents tend to occur when the roads are slick. I was probably a little more nervous than usual because not three weeks before I had been in a rain-related accident which totaled my car. Today we were in our new van.

But my husband was driving this time. "We'll be fine," he said. "Besides, this way is faster, and I want to get home."

Everyday Catholicism

There was construction downtown. The walls erected on both sides of the traffic lanes made me extremely nervous. The woman in the truck who'd hit me such a short time ago had come into my lane and knocked me up against one of those walls, spinning our little minivan into the wall and then across three lanes of traffic. Luckily, nobody was hurt.

Looking ahead, I could see water pouring off an overpass so much that it appeared to be a huge cataract before us. Cars were slowing, but nobody stopped. No signs were posted saying this was a "Low Water Crossing." I urged Alan to turn around, but we were on a highway and there was nowhere to go but straight. He assured me that it would be okay.

The water hitting our new Dodge van from the overpass sounded like baseball-sized hail pounding on our roof. I sucked in my breath and held it until we came out on the other side.

No sooner had we crossed under the bridge than we saw cars in front of us stalling out. A few people had already gotten out of their cars and were attempting to push them out of the traffic. Alan got out to help them, but when he tried to open his door, it wouldn't budge. The water had risen quickly and the pressure held the door tightly closed.

Alan rolled down his window and climbed out. In water up to his waist, he moved forward to assist the car in front of us, but within seconds, water began to gush in at my feet.

"Alan," I yelled, and at that moment, the van began to rock, the water lifting it first on one side and then the other. Alana and Rachel were crying. One of them screamed, "We're going to drown!"

I laughed, more out of nervousness than anything, and told them that we were not going to drown. Everything would be fine.

Ryan looked worried, but was quiet.

Alan waded back toward us, and I handed Alana out the window to him. Ryan slid out of the side window. With the water rising quickly, Alan needed both hands to hold onto Alana, and I couldn't climb out of the window with Rachel in my arms. Ryan was on the other side of the car, and I didn't have time to get her to him, nor could he get around the car fast enough to help me.

It seemed as though everything was happening in slow motion.

Then, out of nowhere, a tall dark man with long black curly hair and no shirt appeared. He took Rachel out of my arms, and I climbed out into water that was up to my armpits. Luckily, it wasn't fast-moving water and was only contained because of the construction walls.

I have no recollection of this stranger handing Rachel back to me, but the next thing I knew, she was in my arms. I turned to thank him, but he was nowhere to be found.

I asked Alan if he'd seen where the man had gone. He said, "What man?"

I knew I hadn't imagined him, but we had to get out of the still-rising water quickly, so I soon forgot about him.

People were scrambling up the sides of the bridge. We joined them just in time to see the roof of our van go completely under water.

A hospital was nearby, and though none of us were hurt, we went there to get blankets while our clothes were dried for us. Eventually, we took a taxi back to Mom's house, because cars couldn't get through to our side of town.

The next day, when we were finally able to get home, Rachel said to me, "Mommy, what happened to that man?"

"What man, Rache?" I asked.

"The one who held me in the water."

"I don't know. I wanted to thank him for helping us, but I couldn't find him."

"He kept me safe and warm," she said, "and he was filled with light."

Everyday Catholicism

I asked her what she meant, but she just repeated her description. I knew then that we'd been sent an angel to help us that rainy night in San Antonio.

—*Kathleen Rice Kardon*

19

On a Cold Winter Night

Since you are my rock and my fortress,
for the sake of your name lead and guide me.

—Psalm 31:3

I finished my last evening shift of the week and could hardly wait to get home, take off my nursing shoes, and relax. I said goodnight to the rest of the girls and headed out the door.

It was so cold I could see the ice crystals in the air. As I approached my car, I saw one of my coworkers standing by the bus stop. I thought it would only take a couple of extra minutes to give her a ride home, and besides, it was too cold to be standing outside on the coldest night in January. I didn't know where she lived, but I was confident I would be able to find my way home from her house.

We chatted about our evening of work as I drove, and before we knew it, we arrived at her house. As she headed up the steps to her door she turned around. "Do you know how to get to your house from here?"

I assured her I would be okay. "How hard can it be? I'll just backtrack the way I came."

I started driving. Nothing looked familiar, but at first that didn't bother me since I'd never been to this neighborhood before. I kept driving, and soon I sensed that something was wrong. I recognized nothing, not the neighborhoods, not even the street names. I told myself to stay calm. I was sure I would find a familiar street and I'd soon be home snuggled in my bed.

I drove. I was beyond neighborhoods. I was beyond streets. I was even beyond streetlights. I no longer knew if I was heading away from town or back toward town. I crossed over two bridges that I didn't remember crossing earlier. Even though I was the only person in the car, I was embarrassed. How could I be so stupid? My husband would be worried about me and wondering where I was. I looked down at my watch. It was now 2:30 a.m. I'd left work at 11:30 p.m.

I truly was in the middle of nowhere. How could I get myself in such a mess?

I stopped the car and turned off the ignition. I thought I'd better take stock of my situation. It was one of the coldest nights we'd had. My gas gauge was slowly going down. What should I do? I could keep driving, but with no sense of where I was going?

I could stop my car and conserve what gas I had left and wait to be found. I would be able to start it throughout the night to warm myself with the gas that was remaining.

In total defeat I put my head down on the steering wheel and asked for help. My heartfelt prayer came from the deepest part of me. "Please God, help me get out of this mess." I was going through a difficult time at that stage of my life and had lost a lot of my faith. As I look back on it, I realize that I was praying not only for my "physical being" that was lost, but also my lost "emotional being."

I lifted my head. I saw a shadow down the road in front of me. It hadn't been there before. I turned my headlights on. It was a car. It was not running but just sitting there in total darkness. I drove a little closer. There was a silhouette of a person sitting in this car!

What was a car doing in the middle of nowhere at 2:30 in the morning? Was this the answer to my prayer?

Hesitantly, I got out of my car and knocked on the window of the other car. An elderly man slowly rolled his window down. He did not say a word.

I said, "I'm lost and don't know how to get back into town."

In silence, he rolled his window up, turned the ignition on, and started driving.

I ran back to my car, praying to God that I was following someone trustworthy, and I drove behind him.

I followed that car … in faith.

Finally I recognized a familiar street. As I turned to head home, I lost sight of my guardian angel. I knew in my heart this was a miracle. As I pulled into my driveway, the warning light for my gas tank turned on.

This was such an amazing experience for me, and so very personal, that for many years I did not tell anyone what happened. It gave me hope, it gave me strength, and it confirmed for me that miracles do happen. After this experience, I prayed more often and believed that God was truly in my life. I only needed to "ask." When I finally told my story to someone, she wisely pointed out that perhaps I was the answer to that old man's prayer as well. Why was he just sitting there in the middle of the night, in the middle of nowhere, with his engine off? Maybe he was saying a prayer also, asking God to give an old man a purpose in life. It truly made me think … life is a circle … and perhaps we helped each other.

—*Debra Manford*

20

Are You Catholic?

He that does good to another, does good also to himself.

—Lucius Annaeus Seneca

Ever since I can remember I have loved books. Having come from a family of educators and avid readers, I grew up believing that books can change the world and put us in touch with the most significant questions and most enduring answers.

Following graduation from the University of Notre Dame with a degree in English and philosophy, I worked in a bookstore for minimum wage and sent out resumes to publishers hoping to land a job as an editor. I finally got a call from the director of the Chicago-based Catholic publishing house, Loyola Press, asking me to interview for an editorial position. The pay was low and I was not sure I wanted to edit religious books, but I had grown up a Cubs fan and loved the idea of living near Wrigley Field, catching ball games, and getting paid to read. So I did the interview, they made an offer, and I accepted right on the spot.

After my first few months, my boss walked into my office and said, "Langford, I've got an important project for you. It's a book called *The Catholic Tradition Before and After Vatican II: 1878-1993*, and I think you're ready for it." At that point I had only taken an editing class at the University of Chicago, assisted other editors with their work, and handled only one project on my own. My only fear now was that my boss would figure out that I did not know much about the Catholic tradition and had no right to edit this book!

Throughout that fall and winter, I devoted most of my time and energy to that project. I was determined to learn about the Catholic tradition while making the book letter-perfect.

The day before the project was due to the printer, I took the galley pages home for one last review. I ended up pulling an all-nighter.

The next morning, overly tired and grumpy, I waited in freezing snow for the 152 Addison bus to pick me up for work. As the dime-sized flakes fell with increasing intensity, I retreated deeper inside myself. Eventually the groan of an approaching bus startled me back to the moment at hand, and I squinted to make out the number "152" against the blurry backdrop of the Chicago skyline. Soon I'd be on my way to work, and soon after that I'd be mailing the manuscript to the printer.

When the bus finally pulled up to my corner, I saw a middle-aged man coming forward with an elderly woman clutching his arm. I thought about shoving my way past them but decided my kind act for the day would be getting out of the way so this other man could perform his kind act for the day. Within a minute, the man had deposited his delicate cargo on the corner and reboarded the bus. I started to follow in his path when I heard the elderly woman plead, "Oh my, it is so icy today, I don't know if I'll be able to make it to the hospital just down the street."

It was one of those moments when you want to pretend that you did not hear a plea for help so that you can just go about your business.

But I had heard it.

With one foot on the first step of the bus and the other on the curb, I looked at the half-smiling driver, then my watch, and finally the gray-haired woman.

Everyday Catholicism

In my bag sat the typeset pages to *The Catholic Tradition*. Chapters on peace and justice seemed to be whispering to me, "What are you going to do?"

In a great John Wayne-style moment, I looked at the bus driver and said, "Go on without me." He smiled, shut the door, and zoomed off. I turned back and offered the woman my arm as the exhaust fumes engulfed us.

"Thank you so much, young man," the elderly woman said in a half-fake tone of surprise. "Normally I make this walk by myself, but today it's too dangerous."

"No problem," I said, stifling a grumble.

Saint Joseph Hospital was just down the street from my apartment. I'd passed it many times. But that day it seemed miles away as measured by our cautiously teeny steps on the snow-hidden glaze of ice. Gradually, I gave up trying to sneak peeks at my watch and fantasizing about throwing this woman over my shoulder and running her to her destination. I simply resolved to enjoy my time with this seemingly fragile soul. "My name is Frances," she offered.

Salutations out of the way, Frances and I chatted a little about the weather, my job as an editor, and our mutual love of Chicago. About halfway to the hospital, Frances asked, "Can we stop here a minute so I can catch my breath?" Though I wanted to say sarcastically, "Gosh, I'm glad you said it first because we've been sprinting like marathon runners!" I thought it better to hold onto her arm and tell her to take her time.

Without warning, she looked at me and asked, "Are you Catholic?"

The question caught me off guard. I'd been privately asking myself the same question for such a long time that it sounded foreign coming from somebody else's mouth. I felt my canned answer making its way to my lips. "Yes, I am ...," I finally responded.

"I can tell," replied Frances with an assuring tone.

From the back of my mind sprang a haunting question I once heard at an Easter Mass: "If you were on trial for being a Christian, would there be enough evidence to convict you?" The answer had continually eluded me. Maybe Frances's "I can tell" was pointing to some truth about myself I didn't ordinarily acknowledge.

We continued on our journey, but my mind sat cold and numb as I pondered what I mean when I say I am Catholic.

We finally reached the hospital doors, and I wished my new friend well. "I hope it's nothing serious and that you're going to be okay."

"Oh," she said, delighted. "I'm fine; I just come down here once a week to volunteer, you know, cheer the patients up."

I stood awkwardly in awe of her as she read the surprise on my face.

I couldn't help but to ask Frances, "Are you Catholic?" to which she happily answered, "Yes, I am."

Somehow her answer sounded different from mine ... stronger, more confident.

After leaning down to hug Frances goodbye, I headed back to my bus stop. It hadn't been terribly long since I was last there, but everything about my morning had changed.

As I caught the next bus, I replayed Frances's question hundreds of times: "Are you Catholic?" It was no longer a theoretical matter. Through her words and actions, she challenged me to examine how my being Catholic meshes with the all-too-often sloppy details of my daily life.

On that cold winter day I felt a powerful warmth that had been stoked by the humanity and Catholic conviction embodied in my unexpected companion, Frances. And as I mailed *The Catholic Tradition* typeset pages in enough time to meet the printer's deadline, I smiled to think that I'd come a few steps closer to understanding the message contained in its pages.

Everyday Catholicism

I haven't seen Frances since that day, but her challenge continues to take on deeper meaning each time I confidently respond, "Yes, I'm Catholic."

—Jeremy Langford

21

Pork Chop Angel

Praise be to the God and Father of our Lord Jesus Christ,
who has blessed us in the heavenly realms
with every spiritual blessing in Christ.

—Ephesians 1:3

I never make pork chops without remembering her face and her kindness. I met her in a gas station on I-75, in 1968. I was young, in a terrible marriage, and I was very pregnant. All I wanted was to reach my sister's house on Christmas Day. My husband and I had left in the early morning. With bad tires and one tank of gas, he assured me we would get to my sister's house. We'd left with no food and no money. I just wanted to feel normal, to laugh with my sister. And I wanted my stomach to feel full again.

The tire blew out somewhere between hope and despair, and my husband managed to flag down a passing motorist, who took him to a gas station to repair the tire. I had plenty of time sitting alongside the interstate to muse over all the events and decisions that had brought me to that moment in my life. I regretted the marriage, but I was also clueless as to how to help myself, and now I was so hungry I thought I would die. It had been twenty hours since I had eaten, and my unborn child was kicking in protest.

Finally, my husband returned with the kind stranger, who drove us to the gas station as the wrecker pulled our car behind. The generous man paid for the tire, the gas … everything, but I was still hungry and ashamed to ask anyone for food.

About that time, a car pulled into the gas station and a beautiful lady stepped out. She was holding an electric stewpot. We exchanged smiles, and I almost fainted at the delicious smell coming from her pot. We spoke a few words, as she moved closer to me.

"Honey, you look like you could use a good meal," she said, her voice soft and coaxing.

"Well, actually, I am very hungry," I admitted, eyeing her kettle.

"You look like you are eating for two." She smiled as she considered my belly.

"As a matter of fact, I feel as though it's been more like starving for two," I chuckled, although I was actually quite serious.

"Here." She opened her pot. "Have a pork chop."

The smell was overpowering.

"Well …" I hesitated.

She insisted and put the luscious food right under my nose.

"Thank you!" I almost cried, reaching into the pot.

When my teeth sank into the tender, spicy meat, I knew that I had died and gone to heaven! And this sweet lady had to be an angel.

She stood there, clucking her disapproval at a world that would allow a young, pregnant woman to go hungry. She was relentless in her compassion, placing her strong arm around my shoulders as I ate, and I sobbed my gratitude. I ate four pork chops, and they melted in my mouth, sending their warm nourishment into my bloodstream and feeding my baby.

She was an angel of mercy who guessed that the burly young man who could charm someone out of a new tire and money was not all he seemed. She could see I was miserable, that I was homesick, and that my baby and I needed help.

"Remember," she said. "God didn't put us on this earth to be miserable. If there is anything you can do to better yourself, do it. God will take you through. He will go before you, and He will be your rear guard."

She pressed a twenty into my hand, then climbed back into her car and headed in the opposite direction.

Later, I asked the mechanic who she was.

"Who?" he asked.

"You know," I said, "the beautiful lady I was with."

"I don't know what you're talking about," he said, with a growl. "I haven't seen any other lady today."

"She was right there with me. I ate nearly all her pork chops!" I thought he was an idiot.

"Nope. No lady like that. And if there were pork chops, I'd have smelled 'em!"

I was stunned. Had I eaten four pork chops? It couldn't be that I imagined it. My stomach felt full, and I could still smell the heavenly aroma.

I asked my husband if he remembered her.

"No. Are you out of your mind? You were standing alone, all the while. I was sick of hearing you whine about how hungry you were."

I felt the twenty in my hand, and I hid it.

I felt the food giving me strength. I had not imagined it. She was real.

There are always those who might say it was a dream. Perhaps my hope fed my hunger.

And perhaps God, in His mercy, sent an angel to meet my needs and make me feel His love.

Months later, when I finally escaped from my ex-husband, I became the first person in my family to get a divorce. I was treated like a fallen woman by some, but with each slur I thought of the

Everyday Catholicism

compassionate African-American woman who shared a loving meal with a pregnant white girl, in a gas station in the segregated South.

She was right. God did go before me.

And He has been with me ever since.

—*Jaye Lewis*

22

Hurricane Ike

Out of difficulties grow miracles.

—Jean de La Bruyère

When Hurricane Ike blasted into the Texas coast in September of 2008, my life changed forever. Ike's twelve-foot surge ran through our house like a raging river, destroying most of our possessions and our home.

My mother's words rang through my head repeatedly. "Everything happens for a reason and for the best." But what could be positive about a natural disaster destroying our home?

While we were sifting through our belongings, an overwhelming sadness consumed me. Why didn't I take my high school yearbooks, my writing journals, or my childhood jewelry box when we evacuated? These pieces of history were now a part of the huge trash heap in front of our home. I tried to focus on the belongings that were saved rather than lost, but I secretly grieved for these mementos.

For years I'd believed that angels are among us. I had a collection of angels made of various materials. These symbols of help were placed throughout my home to remind me of the angels' presence. Ike could not triumph over these angels. Each figurine had floated from room to room and landed gently unbroken. Upon finding each angel coated with a layer of mud, but otherwise unscathed, my faith strengthened.

Everyday Catholicism

When the representative from our insurance company finally contacted me, I was distraught to learn that this was her first disaster. "A newbie," I thought sadly. "God, could you at least send someone who has had some experience?" While working at the house while waiting for the insurance representative to arrive, I noticed an older gentleman visiting with my neighbor. Soon he meandered up to our house. He introduced himself as the State Farm insurance representative and mentioned that his wife, who was part of his team, was on her way down the street.

"I was told that a young lady fairly new at claims would be helping us," I said with a puzzled look.

As if in answer to my prayers, he grinned and said, "Well, she was sent elsewhere, and you are stuck with my wife and me. We've been in the business for too many years to count, so we'll get you through this without much pain."

I wanted to hug him, and I did before the meeting was over. We were blessed with these two insurance reps, who gave me the comfort of loving grandparents at a time when I desperately needed consoling. I was beginning to believe everything does happen for the best.

At times though, my optimism was overshadowed. What were we going to do long term? Where were we going to live? How could we replace all of our possessions? The magnitude of these questions overwhelmed me. After living with my mother-in-law for a month, we knew we had to find a rental property closer to our home. After several calls to realtors and apartments, we realized we had waited too long — there were no homes available. All the rental homes had been taken and our dog and cat were not welcome at the apartments.

In the midst of my panic, something told me to call Katie, my friend and the Girl Scout leader of my daughter's troop. After the storm first hit, Katie had called to tell me her parents had a second home located in Seabrook, which had not flooded, and to let her know if we needed a place to stay temporarily.

I called Katie. "Would your parents consider renting their home to us long term?"

Later that day, Katie called to tell me her mother, Mary, had prayed that her home be spared in the hurricane, and if spared, she'd do whatever God intended with the home. When Katie called and asked if we could rent it, her mom felt that it was God's intention for us to live there.

The best part was that the home was completely furnished, and we had the most wonderful landlords renters could ask for.

I've observed grace in others' lives when a traumatic event takes place, for instance when there is a death in a family. For a short period of time, grace surrounds those closest to the deceased, and though they grieve, they often have a feeling of calm and faith permeating their lives. For the first few months after the hurricane struck, I felt this grace in my life. I felt that everything would work out even in the midst of turmoil.

Whenever I have recurring thoughts like "Why did this happen to us?" I remember the angels who appeared disguised as insurance reps, and the miracle we experienced in finding our rental home. When I look at one of the angels from my collection, which remained intact despite the fury of Ike, I know why this happened. These blessings, large and small, will be with me forever as a reminder that everything happens for a reason and for the best.

—*Dawn J. Storey*

Chapter 3

Miracles upon Request

I call on you, O God, for you will answer me;
give ear to me and hear my prayer.

—Psalm 17:6

23

Miracle on the Hudson

In hindsight, I think something remarkable did happen that day.

—Capt. Chesley "Sully" Sullenberger III

It was Thursday morning, January 15, 2009. I was in New York City where I traveled to work on a regular basis. It was about 10:30 a.m. and snow was coming down pretty hard. I had checked the weather forecast because I had a 7:00 flight home to Charlotte, North Carolina, and I didn't want to get stuck. The Weather Channel website said the snow was going to quit and it was going to be a nice day.

I went into a meeting with my boss about 11:00 and snow was still coming down.

"What are you still doing here?" he asked. "You're going to get stuck up here. You really ought to get home."

So I rebooked for the 2:45 p.m. flight. Seat 16E.

When I boarded the plane, I was on my cell phone, sending texts, talking to people right up until they closed the cabin door. We taxied for about thirty minutes, as is usual at LaGuardia Airport, and we took off.

Sitting back, I felt the steep climb that pressed me against the seat. I opened the newspaper to read the remnants of *The Wall Street Journal* that I hadn't finished that morning.

There was a muffled bang that I could literally feel. The whole plane shuddered.

"What could that possibly be?" I wondered.

The plane went into a really steep bank to the left. It was all going so fast. I thought maybe the plane was out of control and it was over. But the pilot, who had identified himself earlier as Captain Chesley Sullenberger, seemed to get control back. He stabilized the plane.

There was no panic. After the initial gasp from everyone, it was very, very quiet.

I was looking around and listening when I heard somebody on the left say, "We must've hit something. I saw shadows."

Then a little later, someone else said, "The left engine is on fire!"

Even at this point, I wasn't terribly worried. I figured we had two engines, and if need be we could fly with just one.

But as time passed I realized how quiet it was on the plane. There was nothing but the whistling of the wind. It dawned on me: we had no power. We were literally gliding and we weren't very high. That's when I sat bolt upright and grabbed my head. I felt a cold fear like nothing I'd ever experienced.

I prayed intensely. I repeated, "Please God, help us. Please God, forgive me," over and over again. Nothing coherent. There were just too many thoughts going through my head.

Yet I still had hope. If they could at least get one engine going … we just needed some power to get back to LaGuardia. We'd only been up for three minutes; certainly we could turn around and make a safe landing.

That hope went out the window when I realized we were getting lower and lower, following the river. When that realization set in — sheer terror — I realized the likelihood of dying on this plane. There was nowhere, no one to turn to but God.

I prayed intensely. I was there with Him. It was the closest I'd ever felt to Him. I didn't bargain: "If you save us, I will …" Instead, I prayed for my family, my children, my wife.

Shortly thereafter, Captain Sully came over the intercom. "This is the captain. Brace for impact."

There was nothing in those words for me but death and pain. A cold hard reality hit me, and there was nothing I could do about it. I was strapped in my seat, completely and utterly powerless.

In the midst of that utter hopelessness, I was looking forward, as crazy as that might sound. What was death going to be like? Was it going to be just complete darkness? Or a bright light? Perfect clarity? Joy? What was it going to be like in the presence of God? I believe God gives us all hope even in dire moments. It was such a blessing to have that sense of hope and that sense of salvation.

I pulled out my BlackBerry. I wanted to get a message to my children ... to give them something to carry with them through their lives, some sort of closure. I was trying to do that as I looked out the window, watching the water come faster and faster. I put the BlackBerry down, closed my eyes, and pleaded, "God, please let me see my children again." Then, "God, this is going to hurt so bad."

I was terrified, not necessarily of death and what comes after that, but I was really worried about the pain.

We hit the water. The BlackBerry came up and hit me right on the bridge of my nose, just about knocking me out.

And we came to a stop.

I knew immediately we were okay.

The impact was not terribly traumatic. I knew the plane was intact and not broken up. No one was going to be severely injured.

I got into the aisle, and the emergency doors were open. I saw a beautiful, clear, blue day, twenty degrees, sunlight streaming in. It was the most wonderful feeling I have ever felt. Symbolic it seemed, like it was a new day, a new life. A beginning.

I filed out the doorway to step onto the wing, and turned back around to get a lifejacket. No one had announced that we were going to make a water landing and to remember our lifejackets underneath the seat cushion. Of course all the cushions by the exit row had been stripped away and I found none.

I did absolutely nothing right. I did everything wrong, but I still came out of this. If I had gotten out there on the wing, and the wing was sinking, and the ferries were not there, I would have drowned because hypothermia would have overtaken me in ten minutes.

Be that as it may, I stepped out on the wing without a lifejacket. I already saw the ferry coming, and it was like a dream for me. So many things went wrong. But so many other things went right. An amazing turn of events.

After that day, I got at least a dozen e-mails of the drawing of the plane with God's hands lowering it down—"What Really Happened on the Hudson River." I truly believe that.

Certainly for me, I came much closer to God that day. It was probably the only time that I've been intimately, truly wholly there and one with Him.

—*Warren F. Holland*

24

Fueled by Faith

We have confidence before God
and receive from him anything we ask,
because we obey his commands
and do what pleases him.

—1 John 3:21-22

The night air blew on my young unblemished face as our car lumbered along on the long asphalt road. It was a Wednesday, like many others before. My mom, three brothers, two sisters, and I were on our long trip home from a church youth activity. Although I was not quite old enough to attend the youth socials, my mom worked with the program, so I always looked forward to watching from the back of the room as spirits were lifted and laughs shared.

Perhaps one reason I looked so forward to the Wednesday church nights as a child was not because of my burning faith, but because it pulled me away from the troubles that often waited at home.

During these long hard years, my family of eight struggled financially. It was difficult for my father to keep a steady job, and my mother barely earned minimum wage at a physically and emotionally demanding job. There were many times when we truly did not know where our next meal would come from, but we somehow always survived. And we somehow always made it to church every Wednesday and Sunday.

Everyday Catholicism

On this particular Wednesday, we all piled into the car and drove the thirty long miles from our old wood-frame home in the secluded country to civilization, to church. My mother must have known that she was low on gas and lower on money, but her determination overpowered her logic.

There we were on our way home from church on a dark empty road somewhere between civilization and home, and our 1980 Ford station wagon stalled, then rolled to a dead stop.

We sat there for a few minutes that seemed more like hours, while my mother frantically tried to restart the car. I sensed her nervousness and felt fear creep into the car. There we sat, long before the days of cell phones, completely alone. I can only imagine some of the thoughts that crept through her mind. My dad was out of town. No one would even realize we were in trouble. We could sit there all night. Finally, Mom turned around and looked over the back seat to where all six of the children were piled together.

"Kids," she said softly, but intently, "we are going to have to pray."

None of us asked questions. We were a family that relied heavily on prayer. However, in that intense moment, we all knew that this prayer was different from the ones that we said safely kneeling by our beds. Each one of us seemed to take on his or her shoulders the responsibility of the family's safety. As a child, sitting there in that car with my hands folded tightly and tears streaming down my cheeks, I prayed harder than I ever had before.

We pleaded out loud, fully convinced that Someone out there was aware of us. I cannot recall how long we prayed, but I can easily recall the feeling of peace that came over us like a warm blanket. We stopped praying, raised our bowed heads, and looked up at each other.

My mother smiled sweetly and reassuringly and slowly moved her hand toward the key. She clicked the key just enough to make the gauge lights come on. Our eyes locked on the needle that seemed to tauntingly hang there below the "E." Full of hope, we all watched intently, waiting for my mom to try to start the car. Just then, before she could turn the key, the needle on which all eyes were locked began to move up. Slowly, before our amazed and frightened eyes, the needle moved above the "E."

Mom glanced back at us with a look of amazement that soon turned to gratitude and joy. She quickly turned the key, started the car and drove all the way down that lonely road safely to our driveway.

We did not speak of the incident on the ride home or the next day. We did not need to. The next morning, as my mom poured gas from a gas can into the car to get it to start again, I watched, knowing that something miraculous had happened to all of us the night before … something none of us could ever deny. The hope that may have been young and unsteady before was forever embedded in my heart. From that point on, I knew that miracles could happen and that my life would always be fueled by faith.

—*Courtney Rusk*

25

Summer Faith

But Jesus called the children to him and said,
"Let the little children come to me,
and do not hinder them, for the
kingdom of God belongs to such as these."

—Luke 18:16

It was one of those dreary, cold rainy days in February that Portland, Oregon, is famous for, and my mood was as miserable as the weather. Some people like rain. I am not one of those people. I had already gotten drenched once that day; taking my three-year-old daughter Summer to her Christian preschool, so the last thing I wanted to do was to go out in it again. But it was two o'clock and she needed to be picked up by two thirty.

The traffic was terrible. When I finally pulled into the school parking lot, it was quarter to three. I knew Summer's teacher was not going to be happy.

I parked the car, pulled my coat collar tight and buttoned it, then reached for my umbrella, which wasn't under the front seat where it should have been. Someone (it couldn't have been me, of course) had left it in the garage that morning. I muttered a couple of words that likely made my Guardian Angel cringe, and hurried through the lake forming on the concrete.

Inside, Teacher Jennifer lifted an eyebrow at me, obviously annoyed with my tardiness, and pointed down the hallway. Summer was bent over a table, working to finish a painting.

"Hi Mommy," she chirped.

"Come on, honey," I called. "We're late. Teacher Jennifer wants to go home."

She held up her artwork. "Look! I drawed it for you!"

I took the paper and squinted impatiently at it. "Uh-huh. Good." I nodded and handed her coat to her. She put the picture down and folded her arms.

She wasn't going anywhere until I apologized. And it better be believable.

"It's wonderful!" I gushed. "Best one you ever did!"

She finally nodded and obediently held out her arms for her jacket. Outside, the rain was now a freezing, nearly sideways sheet. Both of us were soaked by the time we got to the car.

"It's wainin," Summer observed from her car seat behind me.

"No kidding," I said, drying my dripping hair with a handful of Kleenex before starting the car. I was just pulling out when Summer yelled, "Wait! We gotta go back!"

I slammed on the brakes and turned around. "What are you talking about? Go back outside? Why?"

"My Care Bears mitten," she cried, waving a lonely right-hand Care Bear at me. "My mitten's gone. I musta leaved it in school."

"Oh, for heaven's ... wait a minute," I muttered, backing the car to the curb. Parking, I turned around to lean over the seat and undo her seatbelt. "Okay, look in your pockets."

"I did!" she wailed. "It's not there!" She turned both pockets inside out to demonstrate their mittenless-ness to me.

"Get up," I sighed. "Maybe you're sitting on it." She climbed out. No mitten. We checked around and under the seat and on the floorboards. No mitten.

"See!" Summer cried. "We haffa go back!"

"No! Maybe it's outside, next to the curb." I opened the door and stuck my head out. Niagara Falls poured over what was left of my hairstyle. No mitten.

"That's it!" I pronounced with finality. "You have three pairs of mittens at home, for crying out loud. Now, get back in your seat so I can buckle you in."

"I want my bestest Care Bear mitten!"

"Well, I want a week in Jamaica."

Thinking on that kept her quiet for a moment or two, allowing me to get the car headed for home.

But five minutes later, "I want my mitten!"

Looking at her distressed face in the rearview mirror, I said, "You've made that perfectly clear. Now give it a rest. Please."

Eyes narrowed, frown lines deep, she muttered something threatening under her breath.

"What did you say?"

"I say," she pouted, "I ask Jesus. Jesus will get me my mitten."

Rolling my eyes, I said, "Jesus is NOT going to get you your mitten. He's busy with more important things."

"He will too," she stated firmly.

Once we finally got home and parked in the garage, we went into the house. I told Summer, "I've got a lot to do before I get dinner ready. Go play in your room, honey."

I hung up our coats in the laundry room and headed to the kitchen to deal with the dishes in the sink when I remembered the mail had to be brought in—from outside, in the rain. Groaning, I put my coat back on and stomped down the hallway to the front door. Summer followed on my heels.

Opening the door, I looked hopefully up through the rain for any sign of blue sky. A clap of thunder echoed in the distance. "Oh hush up!" I muttered, and prepared to sprint to the mailbox.

Before I could take a step though, Summer squealed.

"What now?" I groaned, spinning around.

"I tode you!"

"Tode me what?"

She pointed out the door, grinning.

I turned, and, following her finger with my eyes, looked down at the doorstep.

There, on the welcome mat, was a Care Bear mitten. A left-handed Care Bear mitten.

I blinked in disbelief, my mind scrambling to make sense of what I was seeing.

What? How? My common sense tried to reason that she must have dropped it on her way out this morning. But no, we hadn't been anywhere near the front porch. We'd gone out through the garage. In fact, she and I had not been out the front door in more than a week.

Stunned, I turned to look into Summer's shining face.

"I tode you Jesus would get it for me!" she beamed.

Gathering her into my arms, I whispered, "Yes, you did, little girl. You really did."

Holding her tightly, I was overwhelmed with awe at our God who would perform such a miracle for a little child, simply because she stood steadfast in her faith.

After a minute, Summer pulled away to say, "Thank you, Jesus!" Then she picked up her mitten and skipped off to her room.

I looked up to heaven and whispered, "Amen to that, Lord."

— *Tina Wagner Mattern*

26

Escape from Hell

Answer me when I call to you, O my righteous God.
Give me relief from my distress;
be merciful to me and hear my prayer.

—Psalm 4:1

"Engine 18, respond to 1637 East 16th Avenue. Report of a fire. Time out 1935."

Cap was away. Brad was in charge. He and I were eleven-year vets. Greg was the rookie.

The address was close by. If there was indeed a working fire, we'd have to handle it. Help would be a while arriving.

At the scene, I noticed brown smoke wafting from the rear roof area of an old yellow two-story house. It appeared to be a bedroom fire. The residents assured us everyone was out. As Brad radioed our situation, Greg got ready to fight his first, for real, house fire.

I entered and climbed the stairs, stopping short of the landing. With my face at floor level, I looked down the hall … two doorways on the right and a closed door at the end. Smoke had banked down about a third of the way. I took a mental snapshot.

Back at the front door, Brad was ready to make entry. Greg was still nervously making gear adjustments. I saw myself in him. I knew he'd be telling this story one day. Without Cap, there was no time for the usual training. We needed to knock this fire down and out. I took the line that would guide us back out from Greg. "Get your mask on and let's go."

Smoke darkened all but a foot from the floor now. Visibility grew worse and heat increased as we moved forward. The door at the end of the hallway had no knob — something was lurking — waiting to pounce. I removed a glove and touched the door. It was plenty hot. We could hear fire consuming the house around us.

Brad hollered, "Get ready, I'm gonna kick it in."

On my knees with Greg in tow, I yelled, "Ready; do it!"

One hard kick set the door ajar. Angry flames reached through. One more thrust and the door flew open.

I leaned in and opened the nozzle full blast. The volume of water should have choked the fire, but it raged on, roaring about my head. "Force yourself to hold and fight this beast," I thought. My head was in the mouth of this dragon and it was about to bite down when the life force within possessed me and I bolted back. "I've got to get out. Get out! Get out!" I commanded.

I left the nozzle running in the doorway. Through my ear tabs and hood my ears were burning and the penetrating heat was taking my breath. When I bolted, I sent Greg rolling like a billiard ball into a side pocket.

Out of the flames and perhaps ten feet down the hallway, I was in total darkness. At that point I heard a desperate voice cry out, "No, No, No!" One of my buddies was charging me to come back because the hose was doing the job, or one of them was in trouble. I turned and after a few steps was back in the blinding flames.

Then the building exploded.

For a second everything went bright white, then slammed together again with a fierce shudder. Orange and black spun like a tornado. The explosion ruptured my store of strength and erased my mental image of the interior. I hadn't come in contact with anyone on my return. I instinctively knew I had to use what energy I could muster to get out of the bowels of this monster.

One step and I ran into the wall. The explosion had turned me sideways.

A hurried over-correction caused me to run into the opposite wall.

My helmet was falling off because it was melting and the straps had burned off. As I grabbed for it, I collapsed. I knew I had only seconds to live if I couldn't get out immediately. I thought, "Where's the way out?" An answer followed. "You're not getting out. You might as well take your mask off and die in a hurry."

I tried to ward off that enemy, but gave out after crawling just a few feet.

Pressed against the right side wall, all I could see was the raging orange and black storm.

All I could hear was the victory roar of the dragon.

All I could feel was my flesh burning.

Like a View-Master picture wheel, the face of my pretty wife rolled before me. I said, "Find our little boy a father. He'll need a man in his life. I love you." Then my older son to whom I said, "Go to college. It's all prepared for you." Next my sweet little girl; we smiled and exchanged love eye to eye. Lastly my little buddy. "I'll always love you, Buddy."

I knew my face piece would melt any second, but my thought was, "I'm not dead yet." My training reminded me that I had an obligation to fight to survive.

I'd had other training as well. As I pushed myself to hands and knees, I drew a hot labored breath and uttered the name, "Jesus!"

In that instant the roaring ceased. The terror dissipated. The pain dissolved. The fear vanished.

Despite the dragon's blazing rage, I was at total peace.

A soothing voice spoke, "Over here," and I began crawling in that direction. As if someone lifted the corner of a curtain, the fury of orange and black turned into white light. I lunged into the light and found myself sliding down the stairs and rolling out the door.

My crew doused me with water and with my first breath of fresh air I exhaled, "Thank you Jesus!"

Brad and Greg had followed my command and crawled out following the line. Once outside and seeing I wasn't there, the same loyalty that drew me back in for him, drew Brad back in for me. He was trying to scale up the stairs at the same moment I was sliding down them. But he neither heard nor saw me rolling out. Back outside, he was astonished to see me. He approached and said, "Herm, I thought we bought it that time."

We soon learned that the fire was a work of arson that started in the basement. I had only been throwing water through the top of the flames. When the first firefighter of the next company opened the back door and stepped inside, he fell through the floor and hurt his back. As his buddy pulled him out of the flaming hole, the back pain had caused him to cry out, "No, No, No!" The rush of air from that back door being opened fed the fire and caused the explosion.

With my burns and bandages, my wife didn't recognize me, but my escape from hell was just a part of my miracle. My healing was swift. Only skin grafts on my arms reveal I was ever burned. It's the badge of the good Lord's miracle that saved me.

—*Herchel E. Newman*

27

My Gift from God

*The Lord will command His loving kindness in the daytime,
and in the night His song shall be with me—
A prayer to the God of my life.*

—Psalm 42:8

I sat at the stoplight, staring at the sign in front of a small church crowded between a diner and a park-and-ride on a four-lane highway. It was hardly noticeable when driving forty-five miles an hour in a rush to get somewhere. Yet this church had personality. They always posted one-line zingers to get people's attention. Today it read, "If you feel God is not by your side ... guess who moved?"

I sat staring at the sign. It was true. I'd moved. What I didn't understand was, how did I move? When? I didn't purposefully walk away. I didn't say, "That's it. I'm done." Yet one day I woke up saying, "Where did He go?"

As my car proceeded through the green light, I decided it was time to have a talk with God. I used to talk to Him all the time. Typically, it was a daily conversation asking for guidance or help. I'd talk about the safety and health of my friends, family, and even strangers. But, that evening as I lay in my bed looking up through the dark, I decided to talk to God about me and only me.

"God, I don't feel You. Are You still there? I feel so disconnected. It's like You're not around anymore. What happened?"

I lay waiting for a magical answer. Silence.

I continued. "Okay, listen. I don't feel You. I need to know You're here. So if You could just do something. Do something so I know You are by my side. God, if You are here, give me a gift."

My immediate response to my own words was, "What kind of stupid thing is that to say? I'm asking God for a gift. A gift, of all things, not a sign, not help, not guidance, but a gift?"

I lay in bed thinking "Yeah, that's it. Feeling a little disconnected? Ask for stuff!"

I fell asleep feeling even farther away than before.

The next morning I rolled out of bed and headed for the shower. I had a child to get ready for school. I had clients waiting for me. I had yet another networking event that evening. My conversation with God was quickly lost in life.

A few weeks passed.

I stopped at my post office box on my way to the office, grabbed my mail and found a little yellow slip saying I had a package. I went to the counter to pick up my latest software purchase or client package. I looked at the sender's name. Carmen Cardwell. I didn't know the name. I checked the address. It was my box number and my name. Feeling a little awkward, I took the package to my car and sat examining it. "Who is Carmen Cardwell? What could this possibly be?" I slowly opened it, praying lightheartedly that it wouldn't explode.

Inside the box was a purse. A pink purse. Pink was my favorite color. I only had pink purses. All of them were pink. Now I had received a pink purse from someone I didn't even know. "Who is this person? How does she know me? And why would she send this?"

I noticed a small white envelope inside the box with my name handwritten on it. As I opened the card a small business card fell out: Carmen Cardwell, Life Coach.

It all came rushing back. I'd sat next to Carmen at a seminar the month before. We were both thinking about changing career paths and both excited to learn what our futures held. We'd exchanged information and agreed to keep in touch.

But why? Why would she be sending me a gift after our brief meeting at the seminar?

I opened the tiny card. It read, "Diana, I found this pink purse. I originally bought it for me. But God has placed it in my heart to give it to you."

I sat, holding my gift from God.

—*Diana DeAndrea-Kohn*

28

The Cycle of Total Surrender

Listen to my cry for help, my King and my God, for to you I pray.

—Psalm 5:2

The infertility specialist gave me a sad, heavy look as he shook his head back and forth. "I know this is very hard for you," he said regretfully. "I'm sorry."

After six and a half years of infertility, my most recent test results confirmed a disappointing prognosis—pregnancy looked impossible.

A lump grew in my throat.

I couldn't believe I was hearing this. I wondered, "Is my quest to have a baby over? Can nothing else be done?"

"Let me talk to the doctor and have him give you a call when he returns from his conference," my doctor's partner continued.

Choking back my emotions, I asked to leave a note for my doctor. "I would appreciate a call from him about my chances. I don't want to become addicted to the infertility process and chase after something that's not medically achievable. The shots and all the driving are wearing me out. It's not worth making trips here each month if it's fruitless."

"I understand," he consoled in a gentle voice.

Over the previous year, I had journeyed over 6,000 miles in round trips from my home to the infertility specialist's office. Data collected from ultrasounds, blood samples, and numerous other tests showed more than one problem. While most women ovulated monthly, my ovaries either released an egg too small, too early, or did not release one at all. Also, for reasons unknown, cells from my uterine lining flowed up through my fallopian tubes into my abdominal cavity, then attached and grew on my ovaries and other organs, causing scar tissue and severe hormonal imbalance. The condition, called endometriosis, affects ten to fifteen percent of women during their reproductive years.

I cried the whole way home. I lifted up my pain to God. "I may never be able to be pregnant and have a baby. Oh Lord, is this it? Did I get this far only to learn my body's not cut out to have children? You've allowed me to get some answers, but now what? Help me. I'm turning this situation to You. There's nowhere to go. Nothing is impossible with You."

When I arrived home, my husband noticed the shaken expression on my face immediately. Trying to maintain my composure, I explained the results of the blood work. I could barely blubber out the rest of my words. "I can't take this anymore. It's obvious to me that I'm not getting anywhere. Maybe we're going down the wrong path and should proceed with adoption."

Brian listened quietly and put his arm around me. "I think we should wait and see what the doctor says, Sweetheart, then make some decisions from there," he offered. "I kept thinking they would give you a shot of something and everything would be okay." He swallowed hard. "This is so frustrating and I don't know why it's happening to us, but you have to have hope."

Hope? A solitary word with so much weight. The doctor did not have much of it to give me this morning.

I was sinking, and Brian tried to help me hang on. Yes, I have to have hope, I thought, and faith. I have to accept however God wants things to be.

"You're right," I muttered. "We've prayed about this. It's all in God's hands."

Brian held me until I calmed down. My solace, however, lasted only a few minutes. As I retreated to our bedroom, I closed the door, held my drenched face in my hands, and cried out, "Lord, please give me a sign to show me if I should go on, or stop and proceed with adoption. We want to raise children to honor You."

I continued to grieve over the next week. I would tell myself, "I'm not going to break down again. I've already sobbed my soul out. There's nothing left. The Lord is in control. I want His will." Looking forward to God's future plan, I embraced a renewed outlook and surrendered to new possibilities. Maybe the baby we were praying for would come through adoption.

Uncharacteristically, my doctor waited to respond to my note until he met with me. "I didn't want to make any judgments until I saw the results of this latest cycle," he explained. "An egg was released this month …"

"I'm not surprised …" I casually interrupted, unimpressed with my body's performance. "It's done that before."

"… and your blood work was excellent for the first time since we've seen you. In fact, we ran it twice because we thought you might be pregnant."

"Really?" My whole body popped up in surprise, stunned at the one response I had not considered. "I've been praying for a sign about going forward," I blurted out. "That's incredible!"

"I think you got your sign," he affirmed with a warm smile. He showed me the radical difference between this month and previous months. The progesterone blood draw results were three times higher than ever before. My chances for getting pregnant were dramatically improving, but still not certain.

Over the next few months, I optimistically tried more treatments to once again jumpstart my body's ability to ovulate normally.

But no pregnancy resulted.

My doctor recommended one last cycle of powerful drugs to stimulate egg production and force ovulation. If my system did not respond, I would end my expensive medical treatment.

At a prayer meeting, I begged God to take control of my body. As I kneeled, closed my eyes, and bowed my head, I whispered to myself, "Lord, Your will be done over my body, mind, and spirit."

As the minister and others present prayed, a warm wave of calm swept over me. I returned home and told Brian, "I feel completely serene. The burden of having to be pregnant is gone."

After living with our infertility for seven years, my husband looked at me puzzled. "Are you sure?"

"Yes. Whatever the Lord wants is fine with me," I replied confidently.

I completed my final round of fertility drugs and waited for God's answer with peace, yet hopeful anticipation. I got it a few weeks later after a final blood test.

"The results are positive!" the nurse exclaimed. "You are pregnant. Congratulations!"

A shot of energy rippled through my body as I squeezed Brian's hand. Through God's grace, our past season of sadness suddenly moved to a life of new fulfillment!

Over the next four and a half years, His plan of abundance would unfold beyond our wildest dreams. We spontaneously conceived and delivered four healthy children.

When I truly let go and let God take control, He delivered!

—*Kimberly McLagan*

29

Short Prayers

I call out with all my heart. Answer me, O Lord.

—Psalm 119:145

When I was a young girl, the Dominican nuns at St. Dominic's school taught us to say short prayers throughout the day, while walking down the street, riding a bus, or pedaling a bike. They cautioned us that there might come a time in our lives when we faced a life-or-death situation. What would you do in that brief instant as you considered your fate? Say a short prayer such as, "Jesus, Mary, and Joseph pray for us."

My family encountered that situation on a dark, cold, and icy January night.

That Saturday packed a full schedule for my husband, our three teenage sons, and me. The boys had spent hours that morning building a large stadium with Legos to enter into a Lego contest at the local mall. Although they did not win a prize for their creation, they were happy to pack it into the back of the station wagon for the next event, our oldest son's high school basketball game some fifty miles away.

"Lord protect us."

After a thrilling game, everyone was tired as we loaded up the car and headed home. As we drove through the frozen, dark prairie night, our station wagon suddenly hit a patch of black ice. The car began to spin in circles, out of control on the highway, then careened to the side of the road. It crashed into a mileage marker and began to roll.

"Jesus, Mary, and Joseph pray for us."

The car continued to roll four times until it landed back on its wheels with a thud at the bottom of the ditch.

"My Jesus, mercy."

The windows shattered; glass and Legos peppered the interior of the car. The boys were shaken and moaning, but we were all alive.

"Mother of Mercy, pray for us."

The first two people on the scene offered to take us to the hospital, since we were in a remote area and help was miles away. One son gripped his painful shoulder and ribs; the other two boys were remarkably unharmed.

"Our Lord and our Savior."

A van stopped to help. The Lutheran minister and his family would take the older boys to Denver while we went to the nearest hospital with our youngest son. We did not know these strangers who came into our lives on that night, but somehow we knew God had sent them and we could trust them with our children. The state patrol officer told us we were very lucky the accident happened in that location, where sandy soil slowed the car before it flipped; a short distance down the highway was a deep and dangerous culvert.

I gazed at the Lego stadium now scattered in hundreds of pieces in and out of the car, and wrapped my arms around my family, still together.

"Thank you, Jesus."

—*Shirley Dino*

30

My Mother's Novena

I have been driven many times to my knees by the
overwhelming conviction that I had nowhere else to go.

—Abraham Lincoln

My mother loved to recount the story of God's hand in her marriage. In 1941, when she was twenty-one years old, she fashioned her own novena. For six weeks, she visited St. Patrick's Cathedral in Manhattan every evening after work. There, she contemplated the stations of the cross and asked Jesus to bless her with a caring husband. On the night she completed her novena, she volunteered at a USO social, serving doughnuts and coffee to U.S. servicemen. A tall soldier, or "a long drink of water," as my mother described him, asked her to dance. During that first waltz, he jokingly proposed marriage to her. One year later, she accepted his more heartfelt proposal, and he remained devoted to her for more than fifty years.

Not long after their marriage, my father received orders to fight in WWII. My mother presented him with a Sacred Heart of Jesus medal and sterling silver rosary beads before he was deployed. Dad was sent to pilot a B-17 bomber, the Lady Lylian, over Germany.

As soon as he left, Mom rallied the prayer troops. She wrote to the families of the Lady Lylian's crew and requested that they pray for the safety of the entire flight crew. My mother taught the fourth grade in a Catholic grammar school, and each morning she had her students recite a special Our Father for my dad's men.

My mother added her private prayers to the others. She asked God to please protect her husband and his men from harm; in return, she promised to attend Mass and receive Communion daily for the rest of her life. Miraculously, after an extended tour of forty bombing missions, each man on the Lady Lylian came home safe and well. Mom faithfully kept her end of the bargain.

My parents settled into married life and hoped to begin a family. In high school, my mother had written an essay about how she hoped to use her God-given talents in the career that her heart most desired, motherhood.

Sadly, for sixteen years, she could not conceive a child. Obstetricians said that her chances of becoming pregnant were next to none. She continued her education and became a college professor, but her heart quietly ached every time one of her friends gave birth to an infant.

My mother held a strong belief in the Communion of Saints and in their abilities to intercede on behalf of the prayerful. She prayed to the Virgin Mary for a baby because she knew that Our Lady would sympathize with this particular hope. Mom also had a special admiration for St. Thérèse, the Little Flower, and petitioned her too.

In 1960, I was born, and to honor her intercessors, my mother named me Marie-Therese.

Throughout my childhood, my mother was a fine example of a faithful woman. Every morning, I watched her race from the house, still applying her lipstick, to make the 7:30 Mass. We attended church as a family on Sunday, and Mom would help guide my hand as I lit candles for friends and family members who needed God's blessing.

Just as important, she made God and prayer part of everyday life. I can still remember her dashing around the house with her bifocals on her head muttering, "St. Anthony, please help me find those darned glasses." Preparing large multiple-course meals was a joy for my mother. Before we could partake, though, we thanked God for the gift of his bounty and for one another. At night, she had me kneel next to my bed and pray. "Talk to God just as you would to your most trusted friend," she told me.

I married a U.S. Army Lieutenant when I was twenty and moved across the country from my parents. They missed me terribly. When my husband's military commitment was finished, he received two civilian job offers. One was located in Oklahoma, and the other was in New York, a mere one-hour drive from my parents' home. Again, Mom hit her knees to share her heart's wish with God. Who would have imagined that God would consider Poughkeepsie, New York, such a heavenly place for us to put down roots?

In his late sixties, my father was diagnosed with a virulent form of lymphoma. The doctors gave him six months to live. He underwent chemotherapy and radiation treatments; he fought to live and spend more time with my mother. My parents held hands and recited prayers. Dad lived five more years, long enough to celebrate their fiftieth wedding anniversary at their church, Sacred Heart.

In 1996, my mother was visiting me when she suffered a stroke. She had a choice of two local hospitals, and, not surprisingly, she said, "Take me to St. Francis Hospital." During her CAT scan, she stopped breathing twice, so the neurosurgeon was forced to perform an emergency craniotomy. The doctor told me that she had suffered extensive brain damage and might not recover well.

I went home to rally the troops, just as my mother had taught me. I telephoned relatives and friends from all over the country and asked them to pray for her recovery. I contacted the pastor of Sacred Heart Church, and he had the parishioners remember my mother in their prayers. Then, I brought my children to church and had them light candles for her because Mom always said, "God especially loves the honest and pure prayers of children."

When my mother awoke from unconsciousness, her seemingly nonsensical conversation concerned me. "Do you know about St. Francis's stigmata?" she asked me.

"It's okay, Mom. I'm here," I told her.

Weeks later, I did a bit of research and discovered that her stroke and operation fell on the Feast Day of St. Francis's stigmata.

My mother's recovery was slow. She had to re-learn to walk, to swallow, and to communicate. The hospital's chaplain visited each day, and as soon as Mom could have food by mouth, he brought her Communion. After six months of rehabilitation, she was able to live independently again.

On my mother's first Sunday back at Sacred Heart, the pastor asked her to stand and say a few words. She said, "I am your miracle. My recovery—and life—are proof of the power of prayer."

—Marie-Therese Miller

31

Ask and You Shall Receive

Ask of me, and I will make the nations your inheritance,
the ends of the earth your possession.

—Psalm 2:8

Several years ago my wife of fifteen years and I found ourselves struggling financially. We had gone through college together, started careers, and had two children.

As a veterinarian, I had followed what I thought was God's plan for my life. I'd sold my stock in a very successful multi-man practice to go into full-time teaching. The pay as a teacher is not nearly as good as a practitioner's, and the cut was the major contributor to our financial worries. So I had three jobs. I was teaching full-time at a college in Dallas, plus teaching night classes part-time for a local junior college. To supplement my teaching salaries I had started seeing patients in a back room of one of the college labs on Friday afternoons from 1:00 until 5:00. It was a modest practice at best, and most of the patients I saw belonged to students, so I only charged enough to cover my overhead.

Money was extremely tight, and we were not able to pay some of our bills. It was so stressful that my wife decided to take our children and go to her mother's house for a few days to try to decompress, leaving me with the house and my jobs.

Everyday Catholicism

I called her Thursday night and asked exactly how much money we needed to pay our bills and not be delinquent or have late charges. She told me we needed $311 to make it until my next paycheck. We agreed to pray that God would help us through this time. We said a short prayer on the phone, and then I did something I had never done before. I got down on my knees and asked God specifically for money. I asked Him if He would bring enough animals to me on the following afternoon so I could pay our bills. I told Him I needed $311.

After I prayed, I went to bed, and when I woke up the next morning, I had forgotten about my prayer. I went to school, taught my classes, and went to the lab in the afternoon in case any patients might come to my makeshift clinic. It was an unusually busy day; I saw all of the animals and finished up around five. Since my practice was so small, I only had a student assistant helping me. We did business on a strictly cash basis. If the client had the cash, they paid me and if they did not, I told them they could pay me later. I kept the money I made that day in my shirt pocket. I had always focused on service and caring for the animals, not money, so I didn't even think to count it at the end of the day.

When I got home that night, I was extremely tired and fell asleep on the couch. The phone woke me. It was my wife asking if I had made any money at the practice that afternoon. I pulled the wad of bills out of my shirt pocket and counted it while I spoke to her on the phone. I counted out $310. She gasped and reminded me that was only one dollar short of the money we needed to pay our bills. I looked down and saw a dollar bill on the floor beside the couch. When I had pulled the money out of my shirt pocket, I guess a dollar had fallen to the floor. That dollar added to the rest of the wad equaled the exact amount we had prayed for, $311.

That day marked a big turnaround in our lives. We have never been in that dire financial situation again.

I know this is but a small need, but it was a huge miracle when you realize God provided exactly what we had asked for, to the penny.

—*Gene F. Giggleman, DVM*

32

Ruth and Naomi

A mother's love for her child is like nothing else in the world.

—Agatha Christie

Our son, Lane, and his girlfriend were at odds again. It seemed to me they disagreed about any and every thing. As a mother, I was apprehensive when I heard about their engagement. I liked the girl all right, but I wondered whether she was the right one.

I had been praying for Lane's mate since the day he was born.

Now that he was engaged, I wanted to be sure, and my daily prayer became, "Lord, if this isn't the right girl, please send the right one."

During this prayer one night I had a vision. With my eyes closed, I saw two girls. No mistake about it ... the girl on the left was Lane's betrothed. She appeared as a dark silhouette. The girl on the right was a blue-eyed vivacious blonde in living color with a smile that brought joy to my heart. A vision like this had never happened to me before, and I guess I just thought that it must have come from me. I tucked it away in my mental file, but I thought about it a lot.

As the wedding date drew closer, and the church was rented, I became more apprehensive. I prayed for the Lord to intervene if this wasn't the best decision for our son.

Two weeks before the wedding was to take place, Lane's fiancée fell out of love with him and called the whole thing off. He told us his pain would never stop. I felt sorry for him, but in my heart I knew that God had to be working. Amidst his heartbreak, he continued working on his college degree. Two years passed, and I prayed daily for Lane.

With graduation near, Lane called to give us the time and details. His dad and I talked of our pride in him as we drove the two hours to his college campus. We arrived at his apartment, and he told us to wait while he went to pick up a friend he had invited. Twenty minutes later, our son walked in with a beautiful blue-eyed blonde. I gasped when I saw her. She was the very same girl I had seen in my vision two years earlier! I could hardly contain myself, but I kept my mouth closed for fear I would scare them both off.

Their friendship grew from May to November, when our son called us one day and said, "What are you doing November 19th? Would you like to go to a wedding?" And the rest is history.

Kari is the most wonderful wife and the mother of two beautiful girls. She likes to remind me that we are like Ruth in the Bible and her mother-in-law, Naomi. So that's what we call each other, "Kari Ruth" and "Joan Naomi."

This blue-eyed beautiful blonde is everything the Lord showed me and more.

—*Joan Clayton*

33

Summoned to Pray

Therefore I tell you, whatever you ask for in prayer,
believe that you have received it, and it will be yours.

—Mark 11:24

"Honey, I'll leave as soon as duty is over; that should be right after midnight," my new husband promised.

I hung up the phone, a newlywed anxiously anticipating our every-other-weekend reunion. At that moment I questioned the sanity of our decision to spend our first year of marriage apart as I completed my teaching degree at UT Arlington and he completed his last year of service at Fort Sill, Oklahoma.

I straightened up our tiny one-bedroom apartment, then went to bed to await his arrival.

In spite of my anxiety, I still managed to fall asleep, dreaming about our weekend together. Suddenly I was awakened from my sound sleep with a summons to pray, as real as if it had just been delivered by a mailman. It was accompanied by an urgent knowledge of what to pray for ... my husband's immediate safety.

I thought back to another instance just the year before when I had felt an urgent need to pray for Jim in Vietnam. Later, I received a letter he wrote telling me about a late-night trip back from taking a shower when he nearly stepped on a bush viper. Miraculously, he had seen it just in time. He was not wearing his glasses at the time and the only light was from a friend's tent where a prohibited candle burned. I wrote back telling him about my urgency to pray for him on that very same night. We both knew it was the Lord's doing.

So now I fell out of bed onto my knees. I cried as I prayed to the Lord. Then, as quickly as the summons had come, it was gone. My tears dried and I fell back to sleep, remarkably peaceful despite the traumatic awakening. The last thing I remembered was glancing at the clock on the nightstand. It was 2:50 a.m.

There was a knock at the door. I sat up in bed and looked at the clock again. 6:00. I thought to myself, "Jim must not have been able to leave when he originally planned." Then I remembered the urgent call to pray. I rushed to the door, opened it, and there stood my young husband … a bit disheveled, his right eye covered with a black patch.

He quickly answered my questions. A car going only thirty miles per hour, with no lights, pulled out of a bar onto the highway just outside Ft. Worth. My husband was driving seventy miles per hour on the highway and there was a collision. Our new car was totaled. The officer at the scene said the other man had been drinking. The only injury to Jim was broken glass in one eye.

"For some reason I felt the need to buckle my seatbelt right before getting to Ft. Worth," Jim said. He'd never done that before. Back then, in 1969, there were no seatbelt laws.

"Thank God!" I gasped, hugging him tighter. "What time did this happen?"

"I'd just checked the time. It was 2:50."

—*Sharon L. Patterson*

34

The Power of Surrender

If you believe, you will receive whatever you ask for in prayer.

—Matthew 21:22

After losing 150 pounds, I was finally ready for surgery to repair two massive abdominal hernias. In order to repair the hernias though, my surgeon first needed the extra skin to be removed from my abdomen, and for that we needed the help of a plastic surgeon. For eight months I jumped through hoops, some of them ridiculous, for the insurance company to meet their requirements for this surgery. I had a secondary condition (hernias) which required the panniculectomy (abdominal skin removal), I had skin issues, I met the weight stability requirement after a massive weight loss, and four doctors said I needed this surgery.

Something folks might not realize is that when someone loses a lot of weight, the resultant empty skin can cause all kinds of problems, especially if you're older and your skin doesn't have the elasticity to snap back. My empty skin hung down mid-thigh. I had breakdowns of skin hidden "in the creases and folds." My back hurt every day, all day, and the backaches were killer. The hernia pain was excruciating at times, and the sizes of the hernias made me look beyond pregnant. Sometimes I could hardly stand upright. I jumped through the insurance company's hoops for months, as I was determined to feel good again!

I found the perfect team of doctors. They really "got me." They submitted their surgical plans and photos to my insurance company for approval. A surgery date was selected. We got right up to the eve of surgery, and my insurance company denied the surgical requests once again. They would cover the hernia surgery, but not the skin removal necessary to be able to do the hernia surgery. Even though I met all the requirements they'd earlier set out in writing to me, they denied the panniculectomy, and instead presented a new list of demands. This was the final decision, and all my options were exhausted. I realized this was merely a game to them and they had forgotten that I was a human being. A human being in pain.

On my way to work the following morning, I was still crying over the realization that I would have to live with chronic back pain for the rest of my life. I was experiencing other unmentionable problems, and knowing I would have to struggle with those for the rest of my life left me sick with fear. I was only in my fifties. I'd lost weight to improve my health and quality of life, not to pick up a whole new set of insurmountable health problems.

So I prayed. I asked God to teach me how to live with chronic pain, if the surgery really was not going to happen. I prayed, "God, please teach me how I can continue to carry around this skin that is causing me pain." I cried because I'd worked hard in therapy to climb out of a depression and get my peace of mind back, and now I found myself sinking back into a depression. "God," I prayed, "I want my peace of mind back. I need to learn to let this go. You just have to show me how because I can't do this anymore. I'm throwing in the towel," and I surrendered my fears to His care. Then it seemed like God clapped His hands together, cracked His knuckles and said, "Now watch me work!"

Within the hour, Shelley, the physician's assistant from my plastic surgeon's office, called me at work. Forgetting my earlier prayer of surrender, I again picked up my heavy load and started suggesting things we could try: I could take more pictures, I could do all sorts of things. When Shelley finally got my attention, she said that she'd spoken with the doctor and he had said, "Tell Jeri we're not going to go through her insurance. Tell her I will do the panniculectomy for $500. Jeri has worked so hard, and I want to be a part of making her dreams come true."

I was incredulous. Who does this? Who gives so freely, so generously to someone he met only once? I dove under my desk, broke down, and sobbed. Alarmed, my coworkers ran over, thinking who knows what, only to find me under my desk, crying. All those months of playing the "please the insurance company game" and being continually denied had taken their toll. I could have continued the fight and legally forced them to comply with what they'd put in writing to me, but instead I accepted God's gift.

The surgery was back on track and on schedule. The insurance company couldn't argue with my doctor's compassion. I asked a friend why it had to come to that. Why did I have to go through all that game playing with the insurance company? Why after I let go of trying everything in my arsenal to make the surgery happen, did it finally fall into place? "Because," she said, "you surrendered. When you surrendered your will, God's goodness stepped in."

The surgery was a tremendous success. Thirteen pounds of skin were removed from my abdomen, and all my organs were put back in place. Imagine carrying around a thirteen-pound medicine ball for the rest of your life that you could never put down. That's what I had. But, today is a new day! I've maintained a 170-pound weight loss for over a year now. I feel like a million bucks, and I continually look for ways to pay my miracle forward.

—*Jeri Chrysong*

Chapter 4

Everyday Miracles

Remember the wonders he has done,
his miracles, and the judgments he pronounced.

—1 Chronicles 16:12

35

Everyday Miracles

Where there is great love, there are always miracles.

—Willa Cather

The sun rises.

An exhausted woman weeps with joy as her screaming newborn is laid across her breast.

A father beams as his baby girl takes her first steps.

Parents cry with gratefulness when the doctor pronounces their son in full remission.

A pony raises itself on wobbly newborn legs.

A spider fashions its artsy web bejeweled in drops of dew.

An artist creates.

Clouds fill until they rain their much-needed showers onto the earth.

Flowers stretch and yawn and reach their faces upward in praise to God.

By carrying away small stones, a man manages to move a mountain.

Everyday Catholicism

In the midst of dreaming, a grieving soul embraces a long-lost loved one.

A parent who lost a child feels joy again, and a first day without tears.

A white hand clasps a black hand and we hear, "I understand."

A wrinkled hand holds a smooth little hand. "Let me help you."

A small child fills an empty space in an elderly neighbor's day.

An unbeliever tells a believer, "You know, what you said makes sense to me."

An old man smiles and looks to the corner of his room where a band of angels has come to take him home!

The sun sets.

Everyday miracles! Don't let them pass by you unnoticed.

—*Beverly F. Walker*

36

The Parable of the Purse

*And when she finds it, she calls her friends and neighbors together
and says, "Rejoice with me, I have found my lost coin."*

—Luke 15:9

It shimmered in the distance, a beacon for weary travelers. Kathy and I were grateful to have made it out of the urban jungle unscathed and drove slowly towards the oasis beckoning to us in the haze ... Dunkin' Donuts.

Minutes later we were covered in white powder, thankful we had both opted to wear light colors that day. With heads spinning, high on sugar, we ordered coffees to go. They had a special on the supersized plastic mug, free refills for a year, and after a bit of maneuvering it was forever fixed to my dashboard. Head filled with thoughts of that next donut stop, wondering if the coffee would taste better because it was free, I steered my silver Ford Festiva back onto the interstate, heading west towards Indiana, to our friend's house, our final destination of the day.

The next two hours went quickly, until full bladders and an empty gas tank made it necessary to stop once again. "I'll get this one," I said, eager to show off my newly minted credit card. Reaching around into the back seat I grabbed for my purse ... but it wasn't there. I knew my light brown leather satchel could easily slip under a seat, so I got out and rummaged around. I wasn't worried, yet. We hadn't stopped anywhere, so no one could have taken it. And I'd paid for my plastic coffee mug so I knew I'd had it then.

But after unearthing candy wrappers, old newspapers, and half a New York City subway map, I remembered. With all the fuss getting my new coffee mug centered on the dashboard, I had left my purse on the roof of the car, in the Dunkin' Donuts parking lot, in New York City's backyard.

I don't know why I was surprised when it wasn't still there.

Then I panicked, sure that my credit cards had already been maxed out. But something told me to call the Dunkin' Donuts just in case.

"Oh thank goodness," the clerk said when I called. "We were going through your wallet, trying to find a way to get in touch with you. Someone found your purse lying in the parking lot and turned it in."

Refusing any kind of reward, the shop owner express-mailed it to our friend's home. It arrived the next morning, with only postage money missing.

A few years later, on a snowy Minnesota winter night in the middle of downtown Minneapolis, my car's low-gas light was blinking red and I knew I had to stop or risk walking home. I'd switched purses by this time, to something smaller with a strap so I could always keep it with me. I filled up, made sure my purse was securely around my neck, and drove home.

But when I got out of the car my purse wasn't there. Déjà vu. A single leather strap wove itself in and out of my dark green scarf, like a vine around a tree, but there was no purse attached to the other end.

I searched repeatedly under, around, and between the seats until my fingers were frozen and the knees of my jeans soaked through from kneeling in the slush. Had I lost my purse again?

The Parable of the Purse

Knowing my good fortune might not repeat itself, I called the credit card company and my bank to freeze my accounts.

But I needn't have bothered. The next morning I got a call. "Is this Heidi Grosch? We found your purse lying in a snow bank." It seems I had closed my car door with my purse hanging outside. It had dragged along through the snow until the strap broke. Again, everything was there and the finder refused to accept any payment.

I will always be grateful to those Good Samaritans for the reminder that miracles don't always have to be bigger than life. They can be the little things that hit you unexpectedly and have a happy ending.

I'm trying to recognize the small miracles of daily life ... and to keep track of my purse.

—*Heidi H. Grosch*

37

The Power of a Penny

Surely you have granted him eternal blessings
and made him glad with the joy of your presence.

—Psalm 21:6

Instead of making last-minute decisions for the upcoming Christmas holiday, my family and I were making last-minute decisions for a memorial service. Upon hearing the news of my mom's death on December 21, my husband and I attempted to get a flight home to British Columbia. Due to the upcoming holiday, winter storms, and cancelled flights, scheduling was a nightmare. Eventually we managed to get a flight that left on Christmas Eve.

As I packed, I reminisced about a phone call I'd recently gotten from Mom. She wanted to tell me about a Christmas card she received the year before, from a favorite aunt who had since died. Taped inside the card was a single penny with a poem about pennies from heaven. The verse suggested that when an angel in heaven misses you, they toss a penny down to cheer you. So, it reminded us, don't pass by a penny when you're sad.

What a sad Christmas this would be, I thought, as I cried and packed. As other travelers reveled with joy, we arrived at the Kelowna, B.C., airport at 1:30 a.m. Christmas morning with heavy hearts. When my husband Bill and I and our two children walked down the ramp into the arrival area, my Aunt Karen, Mom's sister, waited for us with open arms. After our initial greetings and hugs, my five-year-old son Carter said, "Look Mommy, a penny!"

For a little boy, finding a penny is very exciting and fun. For me, seeing that penny in the wake of the poem Mom had shared with me, made me feel like she was there at the end of the ramp just as she had been every other time I'd come home. She couldn't be there in body but she was there in spirit, proven by that penny.

With Carter at my side, I shared the poem and our own encounter with a penny at Mom's memorial service. During the weeks that followed, I was approached by many people who told me that when they had been thinking about Mom, they'd looked down and found a penny on the ground. I was touched by their shared stories and couldn't believe the coincidence.

Accepting that I had to return home to Ontario was difficult, and getting a flight home amidst the continued cancellations and rescheduling proved the same. Finally, on January 13, we checked our bags and received our boarding passes. I pointed out to the kids that we were sitting in lucky row number 7. After a couple of hours of delays we finally boarded the plane. The kids and I anxiously watched for our lucky row, and as we slid into our seats, we looked down at the first seat and saw not just one, but three pennies.

The spirit of my mom had blessed me with a penny at my homecoming on Christmas morning, and her spirit bid me farewell on my return flight to Ontario.

While a penny doesn't have much value as currency, it's worth its weight in gold. It has the power to heal.

—*Leesa Culp*

38

Twenties from Heaven

To this John replied, "A man can receive
only what is given him from heaven."

—John 3:27

When I was growing up, there were two movies that made an impression on my young mind. The first was *Pennies from Heaven* and the other was *The Money Tree*.

If only I could find the seeds, I too could plant a tree that grew money, or so I believed. My fantasy was shattered once my dad told me that money does not grow on trees. "That's just fantasy thinking," he said. However, I still remained hopeful that dreams and miracles do happen to those who believe.

My father and I had just come home from church one Sunday morning. Ever since our mom passed away, Dad was the official Sunday morning pancake maker. It was a tradition. Sunday morning papers were scattered around us as we enjoyed our breakfast together.

This day, I got all the ingredients down from the cupboard, but when I went to get the eggs, there were none.

"I guess we will have to make a trip to the grocery store," Dad said.

He took some coins from the jar where we kept extra change.

"Dad, are we broke?" I asked.

"No, just a little short."

I had seen Dad put his last $10 into the collection basket at church that morning. He was always generous and willing to help others in need. However, his payday was still five days away.

"What are we going to live on the rest of the week?" I asked.

"Don't worry, we'll make it somehow," he reassured me.

That is when those two movies popped into my head again. "Wouldn't it be wonderful if pennies did come from heaven?"

The wind was blowing hard as we walked from the parking lot into the store. Once we made it to the entrance, Dad stopped outside the sliding glass doors.

Two twenty-dollar bills clung to one door.

"Look at this," he said.

"Wow, this is even better than pennies!" I exclaimed.

We both wondered out loud how, with all the wind, those two bills just lay there against the doors as if waiting for us.

"I guess our prayers were answered," Dad said.

No truer words have ever been spoken.

Dreams and miracles still do happen to those who believe.

—*Terri Ann Meehan*

39

The Milk Jug

May you be blessed by the Lord,
the Maker of heaven and earth.

—Psalm 115:15

It was 1978 and we were newlyweds. Jon was a full-time student with a part-time job, and I was unable to work in the U.S. because of incomplete immigration status. At one point, our food budget was all of seven dollars per week! Still, we'd committed ourselves to tithing and we faithfully put our ten percent in the weekly church offering, as little as it was.

We bought milk in gallon plastic jugs because we could get money back for the jug, and the gallon lasted a week.

One week we were particularly strapped for cash and skipped our usual milk purchase. We didn't really think about it too much until payday rolled around again and we could afford more milk. But the gallon wasn't empty. Then we did the math. As we added up the days we'd used that milk, and the glassfuls consumed per day, versus the volume of a gallon, we realized the numbers just didn't add up. Somehow that gallon jug had yielded a lot more than one gallon. Furthermore, it had stayed fresh long beyond its expiration date.

The Milk Jug

On the day Jon received another paycheck, there was still a small dribble of milk in the bottom of the jug, and only then was it sour.

God provided for us, just like He did the widow's oil.

—Terrie Todd

40

Our Lady's Crown

Flowers are God's thoughts of beauty
taking form to gladden moral gaze.

—William Wilberforce

Mother's Day has always been a special day for my family and the Portuguese communities throughout the world. Mother's Day falls on or near May 13, the day Our Lady of the Rosary first appeared to Lucia, Francisco, and Jacinta in Fatima, Portugal, in 1917.

All my life, I remember going with my family and participating in the festivities honoring Our Lady of Fatima in California. Daddy was always so proud to be a part of the "festa" celebration committees. All five of us girls had been a part of the celebrations. In fact, two of my sisters were asked to be queens and crown the statue of Our Lady of Fatima at church.

When we moved to Washington State, we felt blessed to find the Catholic Church there was called Our Lady of Fatima. They did not practice the annual devotion, but it didn't take long for us to get a novena and crowning in May, as close to the thirteenth as possible.

We started out with crowning a small statue. Then Daddy and a friend built an altar, which could be carried in procession by four men. On the altar was a statue of Our Lady of Fatima, surrounded by fresh flowers. For a few years, we tried to get our entire congregation to join in this labor of love, but all we would get was the few Portuguese and Hispanic families who knew that constant prayer and devotion is what Our Lady asked of the three shepherd children in 1917.

When our new church was built a few years ago, my sister, brother-in-law, and their family had a breathtakingly beautiful statue built on a platform, complete with the shepherd children and sheep, like in Portugal.

Our Lady was crowned at all three of the Masses on Mother's Day. I had been asked to make the crown of flowers and, as always, I used pink sweetheart roses, my favorite flower. When we went to Mass the following weekend, I was shocked to see the pink roses had turned a beautiful shade of deep red! Father Alejandro, also surprised, told me we had received a special blessing. Interestingly, there was one rose missing from the crown, nowhere to be found.

Three months after the May crowning, the flowers on Our Lady's crown were still dark red and as soft as velvet. I stood in front of Our Lady and asked, "I know I have no right to ask, but can I have a sign that this is a blessing or miracle of some sort?"

I looked down and saw under one of the lamb statues the pink rose, missing since May. I picked it up. It was still soft, light pink, with a little brown on the tip.

To this day, that rose has a special place in the cabinet in the gathering area, where it remains, soft and pink, with the original crown.

—*Delores Fraga-Carvalho*

41

A Very Special Rose

Children are the bridge to heaven.

—Persian proverb

As the six of us crowded into the examination room, the ultrasound revealed Angie and Larry's third blessing was a girl. Six-year-old big brother Joshua and two-year-old sister Mckenna giggled with glee and excitement.

As the parents, two siblings-to-be, and we grandparents departed the OB office, our daughter Angie said, "Joshua, you wanted another sister. Do you have a name you would like to give her?"

Without hesitating he answered, "Rose."

Stunned, Angie and I glanced at one another.

Angie inquired, "Joshua, what a beautiful name. How do you know the name Rose? Is there a Rose in your kindergarten class?"

"No."

"Is one of your teachers or an aide named Rose?"

"No."

"Joshua do you know anyone with that name?"

"No."

Gently Angie asked, "Well Joshua, how do you know the name Rose?"

Slightly perturbed, Joshua stated, "I just know it."

This time Angie and I looked at one another in astonishment, fighting back tears.

Two years earlier, Angie's sister Gretchen, who was nearing completion of her three-year residency in pediatrics, died with her husband in a boating accident on Lake Pontchartrain, north of New Orleans. Throughout her adult life Gretchen had planned to name her first daughter Rose. Joshua had never heard that his aunt, who died when he was only four, planned to use that name.

We knew no six-year-old boy thinks up the name Rose.

We knew his parents didn't even have a rose bush in their yard.

We all knew that Gretchen is an angel watching over her siblings, their families, and us.

—Sandra Life

42

The Fish, the Knife, and Saint Jude

Every child born into the world is a new thought of God,
an ever-fresh and radiant possibility.

—Kate Douglas Wiggin

It had been a perfect afternoon. The sun was slowly descending in the west, casting a rosy glow on the dusky foothills as it cut through the haze of early evening. The river was winding noiselessly by as I cast my fishing line in for the last few times.

James, my six-year-old son, had long since tired of fishing and was leap-frogging over the ash-colored boulders that lined the river. "Dad, look what I found!" I heard him squeal with delight. I carefully placed my rod and reel down on the riverbank and went to see what was causing his excitement.

"Look Dad, I found the greatest pocket knife!" He clutched his treasure in a clenched little fist as he stumbled over the boulders to meet me. It was a handsome little knife, with two shiny silver blades that folded within an imitation wood handle; it was just the right size for a boy to slip into his blue-jeans pocket. "Isn't it terrific?" he asked, his eyes sparkling.

"Yes. You take good care of this knife, Son, and you'll be able to use it for a long time."

I went back to my fishing pole and started to reel it in. I felt a sharp tug ... then another! The tip of my pole bent almost to the water's edge, and the line stripped from the reel with a high-pitched whine.

"James, quick, I've got one!" I hollered. "Get over here and help me!"

James grabbed onto the pole, and together we struggled to reel in a large rainbow trout. It burst from the water as we were bringing it in, and we could see the myriad of colors. The trout dove into the murky water again, snaking more line, and we played it, my hands over James's, waiting for the fish to tire.

Finally, we began to reel it in towards the shore. James reached down with our net as I pulled the fish in close to the riverbank. He scooped the immense fish into the net, and with my help, hauled it up onto the bank. "What a fish! It must weigh six pounds!" I exclaimed as I put it on the stringer.

I cast one more time, while out of the corner of my eye I saw James playing with the fish on the stringer. "Well, it's about time to call it a day," I told him as I reeled in my line a final time.

"Dad! Oh, no! Dad, I've lost my knife!" James turned his panic-stricken little face towards me; tears welled up in his eyes and threatened to spill down his freckled cheeks.

We began to look for the little knife, but the sun was down and the boulders on the lakeshore had taken on the ghostly appearance of large black shadows. We couldn't see well enough to find our noses, much less a tiny pocketknife. "Looks like it's a lost cause, James," I told him sadly.

"I know what. Let's ask Saint Jude to help us. Maybe then we'll find it," he said with a glint of hope in his eye. I recalled that his godmother had told him that Saint Jude was the patron saint of lost causes or hopeless cases.

"All right," I replied doubtfully, "you never know."

James prayed with the refreshing faith and earnestness found only in young children. "Saint Jude, please help me find my knife."

Everyday Catholicism

We got down on our hands and knees, our vision limited by the lack of daylight, and scratched around in the dirt and between the boulders, looking one last time for the elusive little knife. No luck. Sadly, James conceded we were not going to find his knife. We picked up our gear and headed for home, a somber feeling casting a pall over what had been an almost-perfect afternoon.

When we got home, hoping to ease his sadness, I said it was time to clean the trout we'd worked so hard to catch. James wandered over, still a little distraught over having lost his knife. He clambered up onto a tall stool so that he could see everything I was about to do.

James watched with fascination as I slit the trout from head to tail. With a sharp knife, I slowly, carefully cut the stomach open. Suddenly, a sharp "clank" sounded, as something fell from the trout's innards and hit the bottom of our stainless steel sink. I picked it up and washed it off. There, in my hand, was a little imitation wood-handled pocketknife, its two shiny blades tucked safely within its handle.

James nearly plunked right off the chair he was perched upon. "I knew Saint Jude would help me find my knife!" He shrieked with joy. "Ya gotta have faith!"

—*Mike O'Boyle as told to Sherry O'Boyle*

43

My Angel, Carlo

If you seek an angel with an open heart ...
you shall always find one.

—Author Unknown

On a sunny November morning in Milano, Italy, my friend Rick and I headed to the Duomo, the centre of the city, to take some photos. We stopped at a little café, and as Rick stood in line to order, I opened my purse.

"Rick, I don't have my wallet!" I cried. "It's not in my purse. I don't know where it is!"

My wallet held my passport, credit cards, driver's license, insurance, and almost 500 euros in cash. I had always felt safe in Italy and never had any issues with pickpockets, so I was certain my wallet must have fallen from my purse when I'd taken out my camera.

"I'm not going to worry," I calmly told Rick, as we walked back to the Duomo. "All my life I've believed in angels. I trust a nice person picked up my wallet and it will be returned to me."

I am not sure whether Rick shared my belief; I think he was just thankful I remained so calm.

Arriving at the Duomo, the *carabinieri* (police) were out in full force. Rick approached one of the officers and explained my situation. The policeman gave us directions to the Lost and Found, and we followed the route he suggested.

But fifteen minutes later, we realized we were lost, so we re-traced our steps to the Duomo. I decided to head to the Tourist Office, highly optimistic that another traveler had picked up my wallet.

My optimism waned when we were told that no one had handed in a wallet. With new directions, we headed off again to the Lost and Found, where their reply was the same. Two dead-ends.

At that point, I questioned whether I would ever find my wallet; the chances were getting pretty slim. Because I had lost my passport, I needed to fill out a report at the police station. While walking there, I had a philosophical conversation with Rick as to the meaning of it all. It felt quite surreal walking in a foreign city knowing you had no ID and no money. I was okay with losing my passport and ID, as I knew those items were replaceable. I was upset, though, about the little red envelope containing 200 euros that I had tucked in my wallet. My friend Renee gave it to me to spend on something special in Italy. I knew that even if I got my wallet back, the cash would probably be gone, along with the opportunity to spend her generous gift.

Outside the police station, a man in a booth directed people where they needed to go. He instructed us to turn left. As Rick headed off, I paused, debating whether I should phone and cancel my credit cards.

"Theresa, are you coming to fill out the report?" Rick yelled.

An older gentleman, standing near the booth heard Rick and asked, "Have you lost something?"

Rick walked over. "Yes, she's lost a wallet."

The gentleman looked at me and asked my name.

"Theresa," I replied.

"Theresa, there is your wallet," he said, pointing to the man in the booth.

I approached and there, lying open on the desk, was my wallet! I saw my ID and even the red envelope, torn open with no money inside.

"Rick, my wallet was found and turned in!" I shouted.

The gentleman confirmed that he was the one who'd found it. When I looked into his kind eyes, I knew he wouldn't have taken my money. I expressed my thanks and how grateful I was.

I entered the booth to pick up my things, and my intuition told me to look to the left. There in the corner of the desk was a stack of 50-euro bills.

The man in the booth asked if I had everything.

I calmly said, "Yes, all my ID is here and that is my money," I said, pointing to the pile of cash.

He agreed, and I counted the money. All 500 euros were there!

Rick was talking with Carlo, the kind gentleman who'd found my wallet. Carlo was saying goodbye, so I quickly gave Rick a 50-euro bill to give to him as a token of my gratitude.

Carlo refused to take the money.

I grabbed my things and rushed out to stop Carlo from leaving. Pleading with him I said, "Please Carlo, is there anything I can buy you to thank you for finding my wallet?"

He thought for a moment and then in a typical Italian response he said, "Okay, un caffè."

Perfect!

We crossed the street, and I ordered espressos. We sat down, and Carlo told his side of the story.

When he found my wallet on the Duomo floor, he opened it to realize a Canadian tourist had lost all her ID. He phoned his lawyer friend to find out what to do, and she told him to go to the police station and fill out a report. He walked to the station and met the man in the booth, who took the wallet without writing down any information. Carlo left the booth but felt uncomfortable about what had happened, so he phoned his friend back. She insisted that he return to the station and fill out a police report. At the booth, Carlo saw the wallet ripped open with all the money to one side and wondered what was going on. At that precise moment, he saw me standing there and heard Rick call out.

Rick and I sat in awe. We couldn't believe all the coincidences and the magic of it all.

Looking into Rick's eyes, I expressed what I knew was true. "Rick, meet my angel Carlo."

—*Theresa Chan*

44

The Holiday Lottery from Heaven

Set me as a seal on your heart,
as a seal on your arm,
for stern as death is love....

—Song of Songs 8:6

My husband grew up in a large Italian Catholic family in South Philadelphia, with three families of aunts, uncles, and cousins living on one block of Cross Street and many of the other relatives just a few blocks away. Uncle Tony and Aunt Grace lived right next door to my in-laws, Philip and Rose. The two couples were especially close since Uncle Tony and Philip were brothers and Aunt Grace and Rose were sisters.

In addition to being very large, and concentrated in a three-block radius, my husband's family was unique in one particular way: the family had a category of relatives most other families do not. While the family had mothers, fathers, sisters, brothers, aunts, uncles, cousins, and grandparents, they also had a category of relatives known as "the Deads." My husband's relatives talked about the Deads as if they were still alive, especially around the holidays. A typical conversation between Rose and Grace would sound like this:

Grace: "Roe, what did you do today?"

Rose: "Oh, I went food shopping, stopped to see the Deads, and then made my gravy."

Grace: "Oh yeah? I saw the Deads yesterday."

Sure enough, whenever I went to the cemetery with my husband, all the Deads would have fresh flowers on their graves, sometimes two and three arrangements, depending on how many of the relatives had been to see the Deads that week.

My husband's family was also unique in that they had a special rule: If a Dead came to you in dream and spoke a number, you played the number the next day in the lottery.

I came to know about this rule in 1989. Uncle Tony, who had taken over his father's fruit and produce business, died unexpectedly at the end of August of that year. His death was very hard on Aunt Grace, for they had been married a long time and had been very much in love. One night, about two weeks after Uncle Tony's death, I was in Aunt Grace's kitchen with my mother-in-law when Aunt Grace said, "Tony was a great lover." The shock of this statement quickly dissipated when Aunt Grace then stated, "The week before our wedding, Tony came to my house every day and gave me a present. He was a great lover." Aunt Grace then put her head in her hands and started to cry.

As the holidays approached two months later, Aunt Grace was, understandably, a little depressed. In addition to losing her husband, money was tighter than usual and the Christmas season loomed.

At the end of November, Aunt Grace came running into my mother-in-law's kitchen one morning all excited. "Tony gave me the number last night!"

"What do you mean?" my mother-in-law asked.

"Well, last night I had a dream, and in it I dreamt that I was asleep in bed but Tony was downstairs. All of a sudden, Tony starts yelling, 'Grace, Grace, there's someone in the house! Call 911, call 911!' After that, I woke up."

My mother-in-law "remained," which is the word she used to mean that she "remained quiet and said nothing."

Aunt Grace went on. "Well that means that 911 is tonight's number! Tony just gave me tonight's number!"

The news spread through the family with the speed of sound, but because Uncle Tony had spoken such an ordinary number, only Aunt Grace and Uncle Tony's best friend, Johnny Gerace, played the number that day.

That night, I was eating over at my in-laws' house when seven o'clock rolled around. My mother-in-law looked at the clock and said, "El, it's almost seven. Go see what the number is."

As the houses in South Philly are so small, I only had to walk about thirty feet from the kitchen table, through the dining room, to reach the TV in the living room. After I turned the TV on, the familiar lottery music filled the room. The number started to be drawn right away. Turning my head to the left, I hollered, "The first number is ... nine."

"You're full of soup," my mother-in-law answered.

"The second number is a one," I hollered a little louder.

By this time, my mother-in-law, father-in-law, and husband started walking quickly into the living room.

"The third number is a ... 1. 911! 911!" I yelled.

Naturally, my mother-in-law started screaming, and we all ran back through the kitchen, out the back door, across the little yard, and into Aunt Grace's kitchen. Aunt Grace, seated at the kitchen table, her head bent and in her hands, was crying and hollering, "Tooonnnyyyy, Tooonnnyyy!"

As my mother-in-law grabbed her hands and smiled into her face, Aunt Grace whispered through choked tears, "He always gave me extra money around the holidays, and he's still finding a way."

With so many relatives living so close, Aunt Grace's house filled quickly, the coffee was made and re-made, and the story told and retold. Relatives who did not live around the corner called on the phone to congratulate Aunt Grace.

Since that night, I have known that love really does transcend time and space.

—*Ellen C. K. Giangiordano*

45

Terry

Earth hath no sorrow that heaven cannot heal.

—Thomas Moore

I hastily hopped into the nearest checkout line at the discount store, my single purchase in hand. Glancing at the two women in front of me, I halted in my tracks.

"Jan. Charlotte," I stammered. "I can't believe I chose this line at this moment."

"It was no coincidence," Jan said with a half-smile. "There are no coincidences," she repeated, her eyes brimming with tears.

There are no coincidences. Everything happens for a reason. That's what Terry always said. Terry, my best friend, Jan's sister, Charlotte's daughter. It was still incomprehensible to me that just two days earlier we had sat at her bedside as she lay dying of a massive heart attack.

As the three of us hugged at the checkout line, the cashier fiddled with the rubber strip at the end of the conveyor belt. With a flat object, he pried a coin from beneath it.

"What's a dime doing here?" he questioned. "I've never seen that before. How did it get there?" He placed the coin on the checkout stand. "Anybody need a dime?"

After a final hug and a plan to meet at the funeral, Jan and Charlotte left. I rummaged in my purse for my wallet, paid for my item, and headed to the exit. I was surprised to see Jan and Charlotte waiting for me there.

"LeAnn," Terry's mom began, "have you heard of pennies from heaven?"

"Yes," I eagerly replied. "I've just read 3,000 stories for *Chicken Soup for the Soul: A Book of Miracles* and among them were dozens of stories from people who found pennies. They saw them as a sign from above, often sent by someone who is now an angel in heaven."

"Well," Jan said, "in our family it's dimes."

Now *my* eyes brimmed with tears.

Jan went on to tell me about when her disabled son had serious major surgery years before. They had found a dime under his hospital bed before he went into the operating room. They saw that as a sign from heaven that he would be okay.

"And believe it or not," Jan continued, "on the morning after Terry died, we went to the ICU to tell her goodbye, and when we left, under the bed, we found a dime."

"I saw it too," Charlotte confirmed.

I rubbed chills from my arms.

"That's my girl," Charlotte said, her voice amazingly strong for a grieving mother. "She's sending us a sign from heaven."

To my surprise, my heavy grieving heart felt lighter as I walked through the parking lot to my car. When I got in, I was actually giggling. I felt close to Terry again. So excited was I, that I couldn't wait to get home to tell my husband, so I called my daughter who manages our retail store in town. As I concluded the dime story, Christie was duly impressed. "That's awesome, Mom. It's amazing! It really is a sign from God."

I went on, blubbering about how much joy the incident had brought me. As I said goodbye and was about to hang up, Christie said, "Mom, wait. Wait. I just thought of something. This morning I looked down on the floor in front of the cash register and thought,

'What is a dime doing here?' I hadn't had any cash purchases yet today and I had looked at that spot a dozen times as I got bags from under the counter."

So together we blubbered some more about Terry being an angel, sending us signs.

Three days later I had the honor of giving the eulogy at my best friend's funeral.

After telling funny stories of our travels and antics, and serious ones of our girlfriend-talks on death, dying, and going to heaven, I told the dime stories Jan, Charlotte, Christie, and I had shared. I alerted the standing-room-only crowd filling the church sanctuary and lobby to be on the lookout. "Knowing Terry, she's at God's right hand, sending more signs and we ain't seen nothin' yet," I teased.

It happened to be Good Friday. I concluded by saying that it was no coincidence that Terry was resurrected into heaven the same week as our Savior.

After the service, before I could even leave my pew, a woman came up to me.

"LeAnn, I'm Mary. I took Terry's old job when she was promoted years ago. Today I walked into the admin building where she worked until her passing, and on the carpet inside the door, there was a dime."

At the reception immediately following the service, a young woman, the best friend of Terry's daughter, approached me. "When I put my baby in the car seat this morning, I thought, 'How did a dime get in here?'"

Terry's longtime childhood friend came to me at the food table. "Yesterday on my kitchen counter, I found a dime, just lying there. I asked my husband how it got there and he said, 'It wasn't there a minute ago.'"

Terry's sister-in-law Kathy caught me at the coffeepot and told me she had found a dime that day.

Everyday Catholicism

Terry's brother Dennis from Idaho sauntered over. "See this tie tack? I haven't worn it in twenty years, but for some reason I put it on today."

I didn't have my glasses on and I squinted. "What is it?"

"It's a dime."

That next week, we all tried to get on with our lives, whatever that means. I called Terry's husband Tom every day, and we shared our tears and continued disbelief.

One evening he came over for supper, and as he walked in the door he said, "Do I have a story!"

Tom recalled how his son had raked their beautiful backyard garden when he was home for the funeral, no doubt as a vent for his grief. He had arranged for a family friend to haul the lawn waste away that next week. Tom helped the young man hold the two tarps on the windy afternoon, then went indoors as the friend loaded his pickup truck nearly full of refuse.

A short time later there was a knock at the door. Tom was surprised to see the young man there again. "I have something for you," he said. "I found it in the bottom of those mounds of waste."

And he handed Tom a dime.

Tom's eyes overflowed as he told that story, and then he and I and my husband Mark laughed and cried some more and made a toast to Terry.

A week later, I rushed onboard an airplane, off to my next speaking event, my heart alternating between joy for Terry and sadness for those she left behind.

I plopped into my aisle seat and took a deep breath. I vowed I was going to rush less and be calm more, like Terry. I smiled as I thought of her.

Then I looked across the aisle, on the floor under a seat, and saw a penny. Chuckling I looked heavenward and said out loud, "We don't do pennies, girlfriend."

Terry

A few minutes later, still amused, and recalling all those pennies from heaven stories I'd read, I crossed the aisle. I reached under the seat and picked up the penny.

And three inches from it lay a dime.

Terry and God are still at it. And we ain't seen nothin' yet.

—LeAnn Thieman

Chapter 5

Miracles of Healing

O Lord, my God, I called to you
for help and you healed me.

—Psalm 30:2

46

Sarafina

See now that I myself am He! There is no god besides me.
I put to death and I bring to life, I have wounded
and I will heal, and no one can deliver out of my hand.

—Deuteronomy 32:39

I was twenty-two years old and a year away from getting my college degree. Although I didn't know exactly what I was supposed to do after graduation, I knew that it had something to do with missions. I didn't know where or how, but I knew my life would be spent in intentional ministry. With just a year left until "freedom," this was my taste of what life would be like after I took that last exam. So instead of working to save money or just relaxing that final summer between junior and senior year, I found myself in the small African country of Swaziland serving AIDS patients and hugging orphans.

It was a cold winter day in the southern hemisphere, and the sun was setting behind the mountains. My group had to be back before dark, so it was time to leave the hut we'd visited and walk the twenty-five minutes back to our homestead. As we passed the last hut to our right, a voice called out to us. An elderly woman sitting on a mat waved us over.

The woman was Sarafina. Through our interpreter we learned that she hadn't walked in two years and that she hadn't eaten in five days. She was alone because her son, her only remaining relative, lived far away. She couldn't walk to the river to draw water and had to rely on the generosity of neighbors to give her leftovers from their own meager meals.

As she looked up at us with cataract-filled eyes, I saw my own grandmother on her knees before me, asking for food. My heart broke and I began to pray silently, "Lord, what can I do?"

And then I heard an internal answer: "Get on your knees."

"What?" I asked again silently, not sure I'd heard correctly.

"Get on your knees."

As I knelt in front of Sarafina, the movement startled her. She turned and looked me in the eyes.

Then I heard another internal voice. "Stretch out your hand."

When I reached for her, Sarafina took my hand and began to laugh. For the rest of our visit, we sat holding hands. That became an anchor for us from then on.

Sarafina struggled with dementia, and many days she couldn't remember her own name, let alone details about her life. When her mind began to wander, I'd squeeze her hand and say her name, and she'd come back to the conversation.

I visited Sarafina several times a week for the next few months. Sometimes I brought her "pap," an African staple food of cornmeal mixed with water, but usually I came empty-handed. We'd sit and laugh together, just enjoying the relationship we'd built. It was a beautiful thing.

One of the biggest frustrations was not knowing Sarafina's spiritual beliefs. As a missionary, I wanted to know if she knew Jesus … if she believed He could forgive her sins … if she believed He had the power to heal.

Around her wrist and ankle, Sarafina wore black bracelets from a witch doctor. I told her that I believed there was another way. "God has the power to heal you, Sarafina. He can make you walk again."

"Oh," my *gogo* (Siswati for "grandmother") said, staring at her bracelets intently.

The conversation went on from there, but as I left that day, I couldn't forget it. And I began to pray that Sarafina would remove those bracelets as a sign that she believed God could heal her. That it would be an act of faith.

Two days later, it happened. Sarafina took off her last bracelet, threw it as far as she could, and then looked me in the eyes and said, "Please pray that I will walk again."

I swallowed. The thought was incomprehensible. "Okay, Sarafina, I will pray," I promised her.

For the next week I prayed silently night and day. "Lord, my faith is so small. I know that you have the power to heal. I know that you can and have made the lame walk. Please, Lord, touch Sarafina. Let her walk again. Don't let my small faith get in the way. But please, let me be there to see it. Let me see you work a miracle."

One day just as the sun began to set, a small group of us decided to visit Sarafina. It was an impromptu trip, something I felt very serious about but wasn't sure why.

When we arrived at her hut, she was sitting outside on her mat watching the road. "Where have you been?" she demanded. "I have been waiting by the side of the road for you all day. He told me you were coming."

I was surprised. "Sarafina, I did not tell you that I was coming today. Who told you that we were coming?" I recalled some children we'd met along the way. "Did a child tell you?"

She shook her head. "No," she said, placing a hand on her chest. "He told me in my heart."

And then I knew that God was about to do something extraordinary.

Sarafina was completely different that day. She was lucid; her memory was completely clear. She recalled previous conversations that we'd had, conversations about the gospel. "Yes, Sarafina!" I was excited. "God does have the power to forgive. And He does have the power to heal."

Sarafina said something to me, looking me directly in the eyes. I had to wait for the translation, but when it came, my heart stopped.

"When am I going to walk again?"

I stared at her, stunned, with no idea what to say. When my mouth moved and when words came out, they surprised even me. "Stand up."

Sarafina stared at me for a moment after she heard the translator speak. No one moved. I couldn't even breathe.

Then she stood.

And then she walked.

Because of the years she'd spent crawling, her legs were weak and she needed people to keep her from falling over.

But she stood and walked with her own strength.

By the time I left Swaziland a few weeks later, Sarafina's legs had grown quite strong. She could walk taller, steadier, and for longer periods of time. The last time I saw her walk, it was in front of five hundred people. They all saw what God could do.

Whenever I think of that summer, I think of Sarafina. I think of how God did the impossible and healed an old woman with broken legs simply because she believed He could.

—*Kristen Torres-Toro*

47

Warts and All

*And he said, "I tell you the truth, unless you change and become
like the little children, you will never enter the kingdom of heaven."*

—Matthew 18:3

In the hot summer sun of the Texas Panhandle, where there are few
shade trees, it takes time to dig a hole, especially if you're a nine-
year-old girl and the shovel is bigger than you. I don't remember
who suggested that I bury a dishrag to get rid of my warts, but I
was willing to try anything.

The warts looked awful. They spread under my eyes in bumpy
waves and popped up all over my fingers. One in particular was like
a bully, a big angry-looking thing as large as the head of a six-penny
nail. Embedded deep inside the second joint of my middle finger,
it was one wart that other people could not see. But I was aware of
it every time I bent my finger, even to hold a pencil. My mother
had taken me to the doctor to get rid of them, but the warts were
stubborn. They just multiplied.

Just before the end of summer, though, something happened.

I've forgotten every single Vacation Bible School of my life except
this one. I remember carving open Bibles from bars of Ivory soap,
making small saddle bags from brown felt, and the last day, wearing
a costume representing a character from one of the week's stories. I
wore one of my father's suit coats, so big it hung past my knees, the

sleeves rolled, a baggy white shirt, and rolled up trousers gathered around my waist with a belt. I'd dressed myself as John Wesley, traveling preacher.

There was lots of horsing around that day since we were all in costumes, but the teacher managed to read a story. It was about healing, an ordinary person's prayer.

I had never said a personal prayer. I never realized God might be interested in me, a girl who mostly aggravated her mother, who thought cap guns were much more fun than baby dolls, who thought making noise was more fun that being quiet. When I went home that last day, though, I found a quiet place to be alone. I got down on my knees and I begged, "Please, God, heal me of my warts."

The next morning, they were gone.

To this day, I can see myself looking into the bathroom mirror. I see my short hair, crooked bangs, and my fingers touching the smooth skin under my eyes. I put my face closer to the glass. There was not a wart in sight. I stepped back and looked at the tops of my hands, searching around my fingernails.

Nothing.

There was only one place left to look.

I took a deep breath and slowly turned over my right hand, palm up. There was nothing but a smooth joint, no sign of a blemish, no redness, just pure, smooth skin. It was as if the wart had never existed. God's love flooded over me.

Almost fifty years have passed, and the memory has stayed with me like a beacon. I've hung onto it many times.

Some might ask, "Why would God bother with little warts and not all the huge hurts of the world?"

Was it my childlike faith? I don't think so. I think it was all about Him. He wanted me to always remember the scars were inside His hands, not mine. He sees me as His child, unblemished. To this day.

—*Martha Moore*

48

The Miracle of Mariette Reis

This will bring health to your body and nourishment to your bones.

—Proverbs 3:8

In 1942, when I was only six years old, the world outside my house in Nazi-occupied Winterslag, Belgium, was filled with dangers. But inside our home, my three siblings and I felt protected in a cocoon of happiness and faith.

We were devout Catholics who were often forced to worship at home. During the war, there were few priests available to say Mass. Even when Mass was offered, it was too dangerous to walk the streets. The Hitler Youth were known to shoot people for no reason.

In our home, my mother, whose name was Mariette Reis, and my grandmother encouraged great devotion to the saints. They taught us that each saint had a specialty. My grandmother visited us on the Feast of St. Andrew and insisted we girls pray to him for worthy husbands. We also prayed to St. Anthony for help finding lost things and to my favorite, St. Thérèse, the Little Flower, for assistance in anxious times.

One day, my mother was taking my baby sister for a walk and my mother cut the back of her hand on the old stroller. The cut became infected. She had not yet recovered her strength from the birth, and she was undernourished because of the wartime food rationing, so her body was unable to fight the infection. It spread up her arm.

Everyday Catholicism

At that time there were no antibiotics to administer. Wet compresses were applied in an attempt to drain the infection, but my mother's health deteriorated. The local medical clinic sent a nun who was a nurse to care for her and to feed and clean us children. She was a Sister of Charity, the ones with the big white hats. She was a petite woman named Sister Elizabeth; we called her Sister Babette.

Despite Sister Babette's care, gangrene set in, and the tissues of my mother's arm died. She ran a high fever, suffered delirium, and fell into a coma. My father took us in to see her and told us to say goodbye because she was going to heaven. I was frightened to see her lying there, not moving. I didn't want to lose my mother!

My mother's doctor, Dr. Reynaert, was well known in the town as an atheist. He was a rough-speaking man, prone to swearing. He examined my mother and decided that her arm had to be amputated to save her life. He would operate the next day.

Sister Babette objected, "You can't do that with a woman who has four children. One is a baby, too."

But the doctor just said, "Well, I'm coming tomorrow to amputate her arm."

That evening, Sister Babette placed a picture of Fr. Damien face down on my mother's arm and wrapped bandages around it. The nun had been raised in Fr. Damien's hometown of Tremeloo, Belgium, and had been told the inspiring story of his life many times. Fr. Damien was just thirty-three years old when he traveled to the island of Molokai in Hawaii to minister to the exiled leprosy sufferers in the Kalawao settlement there. He cared for the ill both spiritually and physically. Fr. Damien literally embraced his flock. He dressed their sores and anointed them with oil during the Sacrament of Extreme Unction. With his own hands, he helped his parishioners build proper houses. He fashioned coffins for the dead and even dug their graves. Then Fr. Damien contracted leprosy and died at the age of forty-nine.

Over the years, Sister Babette had developed a special devotion to Fr. Damien. So that night, after she placed his picture on my mother's bandaged arm, she prayed for his intercession on Mom's behalf.

Dr. Reynaert returned the next morning with surgical instruments, including a saw to cut off my mother's arm. He removed the bandages, saw the picture, and really swore. "What the hell is this piece of junk on her arm?" he shouted.

"It's Fr. Damien," Sister Babette told him.

The doctor tore off the picture, but Damien's face remained imprinted on my mother's arm. Her wound had opened, and the infection had drained. The gangrene was gone; the tissues of her arm, healthy.

Dr. Reynaert turned to Sister Babette. "Well, it looks like your saint did the trick."

My mother was completely cured. She filled our home with music as she played the piano. She was not disabled in the slightest.

Fr. Damien not only healed my mother, but he also touched Dr. Reynaert's heart. The doctor proclaimed throughout the town that my mother had been miraculously cured. From then on, he became a regular parishioner in the Catholic Church.

After the war, in 1946, my family traveled to Louvain, Belgium, the site of Fr. Damien's religious order. I get chills when I recall the small room there, with piles of crutches leaning against the altar and the walls covered with items from people who had been miraculously cured through Fr. Damien's intercession.

In Louvain, my mother was questioned by priests about the miracle. Formal papers witnessed by Sister Babette and Dr. Reynaert were filed. My mother's cure would be one of the miracles officially listed and considered to support the beatification of Fr. Damien.

Everyday Catholicism

Some day soon, the Catholic Church will make it official. But ever since the night he cured my mother, I knew Fr. Damien was a saint.

—Gisele Reis as told to Marie-Therese Miller

Editor's note: Fr. Damien was beatified on June 4, 1995, by Pope John Paul II. On July 1, 2009, Pope Benedict XVI certified the final miracle required for Damien's sanctification. Fr. Damien was declared a saint on October 11, 2009.

49

Mom's Miracle

And the prayer of faith will save the sick,
and the Lord will raise him up.

—James 5:15

When the phone rang at 3:00 a.m. in my college room, I wiped the sleep from my eyes and tried to comprehend what my younger brother was telling me.

"Something is wrong with Mom! They took her to the hospital in an ambulance. She can't walk or talk. Dad went with her...."

I quickly dressed and rushed to the hospital, scared and confused. I met my panic-stricken father in the waiting room as they checked my mom into the emergency room. I started to cry, and my dad put his arms around me. "She's going to be okay."

I found Mom hooked up to numerous machines as the testing began. She lay still while the nursing staff shouted orders and rushed around her.

Several hours later, we still had no answers and Mom was admitted for further testing. Over the next few days, she deteriorated quickly, slipping into unconsciousness. The doctors determined that at the age of forty-two, she had suffered a massive stroke.

Surrounded by my four younger siblings, my dad, grandparents, aunts, and uncles, the neurosurgeon gave us Mom's prognosis. "She has a less than one percent chance of survival," he stated in a monotone voice, "and if she does survive this surgery, she could be a vegetable. In most circumstances, I'd say it's too late, but I'm willing to try to remove the damaged tissue in her brain because she is so young."

He then asked if my dad even wanted him to go through with the surgery.

"Yes," Dad said, "try to save her."

In the pre-op holding area we huddled together, crying, telling Mom that we loved her as she teetered somewhere between heaven and earth. Nurses looked at us with big eyes, filled with pity, as they assisted my mom in mechanical ventilations. I sensed they were keeping her body alive for us so that we could have this time with her.

During the eight-hour surgery, countless friends and family stopped by to visit and pray with us. We waited for any news, sick with anticipation. Finally the surgeon stood in front of us. Mom made it through the surgery, but the next several days would determine if she would ever live a normal life.

That night I went home to my apartment, exhausted emotionally and physically. As I prayed, I wanted to beg God to save her, to bargain anything just to keep her with us. But instead, I turned it over to Him. I told God that no matter what happened with my mom, I would accept it and I wouldn't be angry with Him.

I slept fitfully that night and dreamed vividly. My mother was on trial. God was the judge and I sat in a church pew, watching her plead with Him for more time. As His gavel came down, He awarded her more time on earth.

I awoke with a sense of surreal peace. I quickly showered, dressed, and rushed to the hospital. I tiptoed into my mom's room in the ICU and was shocked to see she was no longer on a respirator! She turned to me and said in a raspy voice, "Hi hon."

"Mom!" I rushed to her side, filled with a relief and thankfulness I'd never felt before. My mom, alive and speaking, had defied all odds.

Mom's Miracle

Three years later, fully recovered, she sat in my delivery room and held my baby boy in her arms. She looked at me with tears in her eyes and said, "I'm so thankful to be alive."

—*Melissa Dykman*

50

Five Weeks to Live ·

He sent forth his word and healed them;
he rescued them from the grave.

—Psalm 107:20

"It's malignant melanoma," the doctor said. "You have five weeks to live." She was thirty years old, with two children under the age of five. How could this be happening? She had so many plans. Giving up a career to stay at home and raise her children, she looked forward to each day that she could give them—teaching them how to read, playing games, and baking their favorite cookies.

And now this.

All that she had planned would come to an end in only five weeks.

My mother was going to lose her life.

After visiting the dentist, Mom had used two mirrors to look at her dental work, and in doing so she found a dark spot on the roof of her mouth. Concerned, she made an appointment with her doctor, who announced, "I'm afraid I have some bad news, but I want another doctor to confirm my diagnosis."

The second consultation revealed the worst. The doctor sat down next to her, put his hands on her knees and said, "It's malignant melanoma, and it's not treatable because of where it's located. We can't remove it all, and we can't do chemotherapy. We'll do surgery right away to cut out the spot and hope that it doesn't spread. The diagnosis isn't good, JoAnn. You have five weeks to live."

Mom and Dad went out for dinner that night and had the gut-wrenching talk about how my brother and I were going to be raised without her. Then they started making arrangements for her funeral. They quickly put plans in place for how to handle the next five weeks.

One item left on the back burner was the importance of prayer during this time. Mom had become a Christian only the year before and didn't fully understand how important prayer was or how it worked. As she tells it, "This is the part where God carried me when I didn't know what to do on my own."

On the morning of her surgery, before she left for the hospital, Mom's friend, Neva, called and read Isaiah 43:5 over the phone. "Do not fear, for I am with you," the verse said. Mom clung to that Bible passage all the way to the hospital and through the halls to the operating room. Once there, she quietly and repeatedly recited Psalm 23 because that's all she could recall from her childhood. "The Lord is my shepherd, I shall not be in want. He makes me lie down in green pastures, he leads me beside quiet waters, he restores my soul ... even though I walk through the valley of the shadow of death, I will fear no evil" ... then the anesthesia kicked in.

When Mom came out of surgery the doctor said she would be in a great deal of pain and wouldn't be able to eat solids for several days. Miraculously, within an hour of her surgery she ate a complete meal of solid food. The doctor was shocked—and that wouldn't be the last time.

A few days later, Mom went to the doctor's office for a post-operative check-up. The surgeon, normally a man with a harsh bedside manner, quietly came into the room, sat down beside her, and said, "I can't believe what I'm going to tell you. There's only one answer for this." He pointed upward and turned toward her with tears in his eyes. "We got the tests back and there's no sign of malignancy or any sign that it was ever there. JoAnn, your cancer is gone. If I didn't believe in miracles before, I certainly do now."

And so does my family!

That was more than thirty years ago, and in those years we've read a lot of books, played a lot of games, and eaten a lot of cookies. And in those thirty years, Mom has fully come to understand the power of prayer—and the reality of miracles.

—*Heidi J. Krumenauer*

51

Miracle Girl on Loan

You are the God who performs miracles;
you display your power among the peoples.

—Psalm 77:14

The pediatric nurse scurried down the hall shouting in Dutch, "Critically ill child, critically ill child! Get the pediatrician!" I felt sad for that child's poor mother. Within minutes, nurses and the pediatrician rushed into the examining room where my daughter lay. I realized my five-year-old daughter, Olivia, was that critically ill child and I was that poor mother.

In light of her severe condition, the specialist opted for a painful spinal tap. I tried to quell the panic welling up in me and began the first of many desperate prayers pleading for my daughter's life.

My husband Frank arrived in the midst of all the chaos. His presence made the situation seem that much more real. We hugged and buried our fear in each other's arms. Our daughter writhed in severe pain, and there was nothing we could do but wait and pray as they started the intravenous antibiotics. No pain medications would be administered until the diagnosis was definite.

When the doctor returned to the room, he avoided eye contact. He seemed to look through us and out the window as he reported the news. Although I understood basic Dutch, Frank repeated it in English, "Olivia has bacterial meningitis. It's called HIB and they'll start steroids, pain medications, and a specific antibiotic to attack the bacteria immediately. He says she'll probably end up on oxygen and her kidneys could shut down. She may end up blind or deaf." He barely could get the last words out.

"God, this isn't happening. Please take me out of this nightmare," was all I could think. I wanted to turn back the clock. What could I have done differently to change this outcome? Could haves, would haves, should haves. How could she have become so sick? Why did this have to happen only six weeks after our move to a new country? Why couldn't this have happened in America where I spoke the language and understood the healthcare system? Here we had no friends, no church, no network.

Panic ripped through me like a knife. Frank enveloped me in a tight hug. Our fear and disbelief bonded us. I looked at him and wondered if we would be strong enough to survive Olivia's death … or her recovery.

Frank left briefly to make the dreaded international calls, while I remained at Olivia's bedside. I felt so alone.

They bombarded her tiny body with more antibiotics, steroids, and pain medications. They would do all they could, but the prognosis was bleak. She was too critical to be moved to a specialized children's hospital; she wouldn't survive the journey.

Olivia moaned in pain and seemed semi-conscious. Dark half-moon circles shadowed her eyes, and her dry peeling lips remained partially open. I stroked thin wisps of blond hair from her forehead. She looked at me with her glazed-over puppy dog eyes, pleading for me to do something. "I love you, Livvy. I'm going to stay right by you. I won't leave." That was the best I could offer her.

In the middle of the night, as I helplessly watched Olivia suffer, I prayed to God that He would either take her quickly or heal her. In that moment, I experienced a life-changing revelation; Olivia was not mine, but His. She was God's child and He had complete sovereignty over her life. She was merely on loan to us. Immediately I knew God answered my prayer: she would live. From that moment on, she did indeed slowly show improvement.

We felt lifted up in prayer by all of our friends and family across the ocean. We experienced a strength and peace which was not our own.

After a month in the hospital, Olivia returned home unable to walk, partially deaf in one ear, and weighing a mere forty pounds. Several times a day she was plagued by severe headaches that triggered crying and screaming fits. Progress was slow, but she was alive. That was good enough for us.

In August, four months after leaving the hospital, we traveled from Holland to southern France to get some much needed sunshine. We decided to visit Lourdes, where in 1858 the Blessed Virgin Mary appeared eighteen times to Bernadette Soubirous, a fourteen-year-old peasant girl. Olivia knew about the thousands of miracle healings that had happened there since, and she insisted on entering the healing baths. We explained to her that there might be a long wait since there were many ill people on stretchers and in wheelchairs. She would not be swayed; she expected a full healing.

We waited over two hours before our turn. As a lanky five-year-old, she looked kind of strange waiting in a stroller, but she didn't mind. The atmosphere was quiet and serene as her turn arrived and the aides whispered prayers in French as they submerged her in the stone bath.

Upon exiting the water, Olivia declared, "The water felt holy. God healed me."

And He did.

Within days, she began to hold her head upright and walk better. When we returned to Holland, the therapist reported that her short-term memory was back to normal. Her headaches disappeared, and so did her tantrums. Much to the astonishment of the hearing specialist, her "permanent" hearing loss returned to completely normal.

Olivia spent month after month attending physical therapy to regain her walking and fine motor skills. She received speech therapy to speed up the process of learning Dutch. By February, she passed the Dutch standardized kindergarten tests with all A's.

Today, eleven years later, Olivia is a vibrant sixteen-year-old honor student who loves to sing, play classical guitar, and eat ice cream. We cherish each moment of her precious life ... our miracle girl on loan.

—*Johnna Stein*

52

Baby Loren

Seeing Jesus, he fell at his feet and pleaded
earnestly with him, "My little daughter is dying.
Please come and put your hands on her
so that she will be healed and live."

—Mark 5:22-23

Baby Girl Loren was born in Paris, France. Less than one hour after her birth, she was rushed to the neonatal intensive care unit with a heart rate of 280 beats per minute, twice the norm. A rate this high eventually stops the exhausted heart.

Loren's heart was cardioverted, or shocked, back into a normal rhythm. She was placed on intravenous medication to keep the heart rate down and the rhythm normal. But she did not respond to any of the various medications and she received cardioversion several times a day during her first month of life.

After spending one month in the NICU with a rapid, lethal, and uncontrollable heart rhythm, Loren's doctors decided to send her to Texas Children's Hospital in Houston.

The baby was airlifted and admitted to the pediatric intensive care unit that would become her home for the next four to five weeks. The cardiac catheterization lab found the cause of the rapid heart rhythm, though during the procedure she was shocked numerous times again. Diagnosis ... multiple heart tumors. She was scheduled for open heart surgery, an extremely high risk, not only because of Loren's small body mass, but because this type of heart surgery had only been done a few times in the past. Part of the heart muscle would have to be cut away to remove the tumors.

Baby Loren went into surgery the next Friday morning, less than one week after arriving at Texas Children's Hospital. I went about my day taking care of the children who came into the cardiac clinic. My mind was on Baby Loren, and I offered up prayers for her all day as I worked.

The baby's parents stayed at the hotel. They had been told at birth that her chance of survival was very slim. They flew over with her, admitted her to the hospital, and then went to a hotel. I'd learned that some parents just couldn't tolerate the heartache. Hers occasionally talked to the doctor on the phone, but did not come back to the hospital for a week.

At 3:00 p.m. on the afternoon of her surgery, the pediatric cardiologist came out of the operating room instructing me to call and ask Loren's parents to come. The doctor said that the surgeon had cut away close to forty percent of the heart muscle to try and remove the tumors. He said that Baby Loren would never come off the heart-lung bypass machine that was used to keep the blood flowing throughout her body and lungs while the heart was opened.

I made the call to Baby Loren's parents, telling them very little about Loren's grave condition, only that she was not doing well and that they needed to come.

As soon as I hung up, the pediatric cardiologist came in with his head down and said, "They can't get her off the heart pump. So they are going to unhook everything and let her go."

I went to an old broom closet that had been converted into a bathroom, where I spent many minutes of my day in prayer for the sick and hurting kids and parents. There, surrounded by soap, antiseptic, and paper towels, I prayed fervently, asking God to give Loren a chance to know what it was like to live outside a hospital, free of pain and with her parents who could hold her and love her. I was there for Loren's arrival at the open heart recovery room, where tubes and wires covered her body. She was barely visible through the doctors and nurses surrounding her, but I saw a heartbeat on the monitor. She was still alive.

The surgical nurse reported that when Baby Loren was taken off the heart-lung bypass machine, she had no blood pressure. Then, remarkably, as the last sutures were placed, her blood pressure slowly rose to an acceptable range. Her heart started beating on its own. The rhythm was a normal regular rhythm, no racing.

The chief surgeon walked into the recovery room at that moment and called every nurse and doctor over to Loren's bedside. "I want you all to see a miracle right here. This child should not be alive. Someone was watching over her."

As the days passed, Baby Loren got stronger and began acting like a normal baby. After one month in our hospital, Loren's parents came to take her home. It was joyous to see Loren being held and hugged by her mother and father after almost three months of living with tubes, lines, and wires.

When I watched them leave the hospital, it occurred to me that God had answered my bathroom prayer exactly as I had asked. Baby Loren was going home to live. She was free of pain and carried by her parents who loved her.

—*Kim D. Armstrong*

53

The Empty Room

By faith in the name of Jesus, this man whom you see and know was made strong. It is Jesus' name and the faith that comes through him that has given this complete healing to him, as you can all see.

—Acts 3:15-17

On a Friday morning in July, we arrived unexpectedly at my father's house in Browerville, Minnesota. I told Dad that our eighteen-year-old son, Vaughn, had decided to stay home with friends and work instead of attending the family reunion.

The phone rang.

I explained why we'd come to Dad's rather than keeping our original plan. On the trip from Fort Collins, Colorado, our twenty-eight-foot motor home overheated every time we drove over fifty miles per hour. It would die and not start again until it cooled off. We'd dropped my aging mother-in-law in a nearby town at her brother's. By the time we arrived at our hosts, they weren't home so we'd come to Dad's.

The phone rang again.

Dad answered it. "It's a miracle you found them. I didn't expect them to come here today." He handed the phone to me.

My daughter, a student at the University of Northern Colorado in Greeley, was sobbing. "Mom, the hospital called me. Vaughn's been in a serious motorcycle accident. He is in emergency surgery now and the insurance company says I have to get your permission to sign all the papers. And he needs more surgeries!"

I fell into the nearest chair. "Wait a minute. What accident? What surgeries?"

"He rode his motorcycle up the canyon to Estes Park for breakfast. On the way down the mountains, he hit gravel and careened off a bridge. He's in emergency surgery now and will need lots more."

We hadn't thought twice about leaving Vaughn at home. After all, he was a very responsible high school senior.

"It's bad. You need to come home," pleaded my daughter.

"We're on our way." Shaking, I hung up. I wiped tears from my face as I relayed her message to her father. Then I began to pray.

Gordon's clock-like mind ticked off everything we needed to do: call the hospital, pack, pick up Mom … FAST!

But neither Mom nor her brother answered the door. How we guessed the right restaurant on the first try and found them, I'll never know.

With the bulk of the drive at night, we avoided the mobile home overheating. I called the hospital each time we filled up with gas. "He's still in surgery."

Next they said, "He's listed in critical condition."

One hundred miles from home, the motor home sputtered and slowed. "I've never run out of gas … until now." Gordon pounded his palm on the steering wheel and pulled to the shoulder.

No sooner had we stopped than a knock came on the driver's side window. "Do you need help?" a stranger asked. He drove Gordon to a gas station and back.

Gordon was surprised. "The attendant loaned me a can, filled it with gas, and told me to pay when I come back."

Miraculously, the motor home started. From the gas station, I called the hospital again. "He's still critical." I closed the door to the motor home's bedroom, knelt, and continued my prayers.

Everyday Catholicism

We pulled into the Fort Collins hospital parking lot Saturday afternoon around one o'clock and waded through a crowd of high school students to Vaughn's room.

The doctor explained, "We removed his spleen, mended a broken femur, and repaired other organs." They'd also wrapped his broken ribs, cleaned his own blood, and given it back to him in addition to eight donated pints. "We're giving him every medication we know to help him live."

Vaughn woke up and was obviously glad to see us. Then he said, "Mom, feel my stomach." His bloated, hard-as-a-rock abdomen alerted us to more problems.

Within minutes, doctors hurried into the room. "Vaughn needs more surgery. Now! He's literally bleeding to death inside." They whisked him away.

After surgery, Vaughn lay in a coma. "The meds don't seem to be working," said the doctor. "If he doesn't make a turnaround during the night, I'm afraid there is little hope."

Gordon and I sat by the bed with Michael, Vaughn's "blood brother." Gordon nodded off. I tapped his shoulder. "Why don't you go home and get some rest? Michael and I will stay."

Gordon hugged me goodbye and promised to relieve me later.

Around wires and tubes, I kissed my son's forehead and prayed harder than ever before in my life.

At two or three in the morning, I felt suffocated in the dim, stark room full of beeping monitors. Before he'd left, my priest said, "I keep Hosts in the chapel." As a Eucharistic minister, I knew the protocol. I hurried to the chapel, found the Hosts and cradled one in my palm.

Back in Vaughn's room, I told Michael, "The doctors have done all they can. The rest is up to God."

Trusting the miracle of the Eucharist, I broke the Host into three pieces. One piece I placed on my comatose son's tongue. I gave the second to Michael. The last I placed in my mouth and prayed. "Dear God, will You heal Vaughn because the doctors can't? Please take over so we can have our son back."

Then, having done all we could, Michael and I went home. I told Gordon what I'd done. He showered and left for the hospital to replace me.

I'd barely changed my clothes when he called. "Hurry. Come back."

I imagined the worst.

Gordon said, "When I walked into Vaughn's room, it was empty, the bed half stripped."

I fell into a chair; sobs choked me.

"I panicked," he said. "I believed our Vaughn had died."

I gripped the phone with both hands. "Believed?"

Gordon answered, "A scream rose in my throat and I fell to my knees. Finally, I left the room. That's when I saw the miracle."

"What miracle?" I stammered.

"Outside the empty room, I saw Vaughn pushing his IV stand down the hall. He wasn't connected to any monitors. A nurse walked beside him. She said she wished they'd videotaped his rapid recovery because they can't explain it."

I can.

— *Elaine Hanson as told to Linda Osmundson*

54

Trapped Beneath a Tombstone

*"But I will restore you to health and
heal your wounds," declares the Lord....*

—Jeremiah 30:17

"Mama!" my six-year-old daughter Blake's scream shattered the tranquility of the March afternoon.

Somehow I knew that this was not one of her come-look-what-I-found or let-me-tattle-on-my brother outbursts. Something was wrong. Really wrong. Heart pounding, I bolted toward the corner of the yard where the children had been playing. Nothing could have prepared me for what I saw there.

Our two-year-old son Matthew lay in the damp grass of the small cemetery located at the edge of our property, his body wedged beneath a four-inch-thick tombstone. His head was pinned to the ground by the massive granite slab. He wasn't moving. And he wasn't making a sound.

"Please, God, no," I prayed aloud. "This can't really be happening. Let this be some terrible dream, God. Please!"

"Tim!" I screamed for my husband. "Hurry!"

Tim vaulted the low fence that surrounded the cemetery. Though he's big and strong—6 feet 5 inches and 250 pounds—it didn't seem possible that one man could possibly budge the enormous grave marker. But with a single adrenaline-powered heave,

Tim rolled the tombstone off Matthew. Then he charged toward the house and the telephone.

I scooped my son off the cold ground and cradled his limp body in my arms. His eyes were closed and his breathing was shallow and ragged. Blood trickled from his nose, eyes, and mouth.

"Don't die," I begged, hugging him close. "Please, Matthew, don't die."

That day in March had brought the first warm temperatures of the year, and spring fever had hit our family in a big way. I washed windows while the children played outside. Tim declared the afternoon perfect for painting some old wicker furniture. Knowing that wet paint and small children don't mix, I had shooed Blake and Matthew out of temptation's way.

"Is it okay if we play in the cemetery?" Blake had asked. I had nodded consent.

The cemetery had been a source of fascination ever since we'd bought our five-acre piece of rural property a couple of years earlier. Abandoned and overgrown, no one seemed to know who was responsible for maintaining its eighteenth- and nineteenth-century graves. And so we became its unofficial caretakers. Sometimes we'd walk among the graves, reading the inscriptions on the tombstones. Blake was fascinated by the large number of children's graves.

"Why did so many children die in the olden days?" she asked.

"People didn't have good medical care back then like they do now," I explained.

Those words came back to me now as I held Matthew's frail body in my arms. In a century filled with medical miracles, could doctors fix a little boy whose head had been crushed by a tombstone? And would he even live long enough to make it to the hospital where they could try?

I closed my eyes and once again began to pray. "Please, God, let Matthew live. Don't take my son away."

Everyday Catholicism

As I opened my eyes, a strange peace descended upon me. "Have faith. Everything's going to be okay. Matthew is in my hands." Those words filled my heart as I stroked my little boy's soft hair and waited for emergency personnel to arrive. "Have faith."

A Life Flight helicopter touched down just minutes after an ambulance screamed onto our property. "We've got a hot load," the driver shouted to the pilot. "Get him to the hospital as quick as you can."

Hot load? I'd never heard that term before. And yet the words caused no panic in my heart. The peace I'd felt earlier remained. "Matthew is in my hands."

Because we weren't allowed to ride in the helicopter, we jumped into Tim's truck and gunned it for the hospital. But Matthew had already been taken to surgery by the time we arrived. Friends and family gathered in the waiting room. With each tearful hug or handshake, I felt myself grow stronger.

"Matthew's going to be okay," I kept saying. "I know he is."

Five long hours later, Tim and I were allowed into Pediatric Intensive Care. Lying in a stark white crib, immobilized by a neck brace and with tubes connected to various parts of his body, Matthew bore no resemblance to the boisterous child who'd been frolicking in the yard and climbing on gravestones only a few hours earlier.

"He's not going to die. Right, Doc?" Tim stammered. "Tell me my boy's going to be okay."

"We can't know that yet," the doctor answered softly. "It's a wonder he's alive at all. There's some possibility of paralysis. Maybe brain damage. And a strong chance that his hearing or vision will be affected."

The color drained from Tim's face and he collapsed into a chair. I went to him and put my arms around him. "Matthew's going to be fine," I said.

"How can you say that?" he asked, tears streaming down his cheeks. "How do you know?"

"I have it on good authority," I told him. "The ultimate authority."

As He is one hundred percent of the time, that authority proved to be right. Exactly one week after the accident happened, Matthew was discharged from the hospital. He went home with a fractured facial bone, a crushed ear, a broken nose, and a shunt in his lower back to remove fluid from his spine.

"I never expected that baby to make it," one of the Life Flight nurses confessed to me the day we left the hospital. "It's nothing short of a miracle."

Today, Matthew is a happy, healthy teenager. He loves sports and video games and does well in school. The only reminders of his accident are the eyeglasses he wears to protect his "strong" eye and a compromised sense of smell. Though he has no real memory of the accident, he has heard the story re-told so many times that he claims to remember it in great detail.

So what saved Matthew from death that fateful spring afternoon?

Some say it was the fact that the ground was so soft that it gave way just enough under the weight of the tombstone that the child beneath it was not crushed. Others credit our county's 911 location identification system for allowing emergency workers to reach our home so quickly. Still others point to the fact that our yard was large and flat enough for the helicopter to land.

All those factors, no doubt, played a role in Matthew's miracle. But I know what really saved his life that afternoon. Matthew does, too. "Dad lifted the tombstone off me and a helicopter flew me to the hospital so the doctors could operate," he says. "And God saved my life."

Everyday Catholicism

"Matthew is in my hands. He's going to be all right," God whispered to me that horrible afternoon. "Have faith. Have faith." I did. And I still do. Now more than ever.

—*Mandy Hastings*

55

God's Little Miracle

Jesus said to them,
"I did one miracle, and you are all astonished."

—John 7:21

My husband and I were expecting our fourth child. I had a normal pregnancy up until about thirty-one weeks when the doctors noticed there was a problem in the baby's growth; he was only in the tenth percentile for his gestational age. Because of this, the doctors began monitoring me more closely, doing non-stress tests and ultrasounds twice a week. At thirty-four weeks, they noticed that I had excessive fluid around the baby, that the baby's limbs were shorter than they should be, and that the baby appeared to have a "double-bubble" stomach. My doctors here in southeastern New Mexico decided to send me to a maternal fetal medicine specialist in Odessa, Texas (about eighty miles away).

In Odessa, the specialist performed another ultrasound. He confirmed the problems that the doctors at home had stated, but he was able to give these problems a name. The "double-bubble" in the baby's stomach was a condition called duodenal atresia, where the tube leading from the stomach to the small intestine is not present or is blocked. Because he wasn't able to pass any of the fluid, the baby's stomach and kidneys were bloated beyond normal. As long as the baby was in the womb, the doctor assured me he was fine and not in any pain, but that he would need surgery to correct the duodenal atresia shortly after birth. Because the baby had this condition, shortened arms and legs, and the fact that I had so much fluid surrounding him, the doctor also informed me that there was a great possibility that the baby would be born with Down syndrome. Because of all of these complications, he wanted to send me to Dallas (about 400 miles from home) to deliver in order to be close to some of the best NICU departments and pediatric surgeons in the world.

Of course, my husband and I were devastated. We were worried about the life expectancy of our child and about the things that he might not be able to do if he were born with Down syndrome. However, although we both felt like having a child with Down syndrome would be a challenge, we knew that it would still be rewarding and that we could give him the best life possible. We weren't really upset about Down syndrome; we were terrified of the surgery and the recovery. Plus, we had three school-age children who we would have to leave at home with family while we were away in Dallas.

I had almost a week to get ready to go to Dallas, so I prepared my kids at home and my husband and I tried to prepare ourselves. We called all of our family, and we were put on prayer lists around the country. My husband, children, and I prayed every night at the dinner table like we always did, but we really focused on praying for our unborn baby. I cried often, but I knew God would help us through — he always had before.

We went to Dallas when I was thirty-six weeks pregnant and met with a maternal fetal medicine specialist and the surgeons at Children's Medical Center. They did another ultrasound and confirmed the previous findings. The day after we arrived, they induced my labor. After three days there was still no baby, not even close. In the meantime, everyone continued to pray for us.

We missed our kids, they missed us, and we were worried about the new baby. However, God heard the prayers of our friends and family, and even though the circumstances were trying, God gave us a peace that I cannot explain in words. We just knew everything was going to be okay, and we continued to pray. After the third day of labor, the doctors let me go back to the hotel for the weekend and they said we would try again on Monday. Monday morning we returned to the hospital but I didn't progress, and they finally took the baby by C-section.

My little Jacob Stewart Rich weighed four pounds fourteen ounces and appeared to be doing well. Almost immediately after birth, we were told that he did not have Down syndrome. That night, the nurses in the NICU gave Jake a bottle, and lo and behold the next morning he pooped! He was never supposed to be able to do that until after surgery because his intestines weren't attached to his stomach. My husband and I had never been happier to see a dirty diaper! They transferred Jake to Children's Medical Center to run tests to see what happened. They ran X-rays, upper GIs, lower GIs, did blood work, you name it. After four days of extensive testing, they finally told us—not only did Jake not have Down syndrome, they could not find any evidence of the duodenal atresia. Our little boy was small but perfectly healthy.

We returned home after spending two weeks in Dallas. All the doctors apologized for their "mistakes," but I told each and every one of them, "I don't believe that the four doctors at home, the doctor in Odessa, and the doctor in Dallas all were mistaken—God healed him." I believe that God wasn't finished with Jacob the first day they induced my labor, and that's why I was in labor for three days without moving close to delivery. God was still working on him, healing him, and He wasn't ready for Jacob to be born yet! I know without a doubt that God healed my son, that He heard all of those wonderful people that remembered us in their prayers.

Everyday Catholicism

I am a firm believer that God makes miracles happen every day, and that He does hear prayers. I feel extremely blessed not only to have a healthy son, but also to have experienced firsthand one of God's miracles.

—*Kelly Stewart Rich*

56

Irish Wake

Rejoice and be glad,
for your reward will be great in heaven.

—Matthew 5:12

My dad possessed a special Irish sense of humor, filled with wisdom, love, and great trust in God and His care for us all. As my father's cancer advanced beyond all hope, in the winter of 1984, Dad set about putting his life affairs in order.

After his last surgery, when the doctor told him he could do nothing more to stop the cancer, Dad pondered this for a moment, looked the doctor in the eye, and said, "Well now, it's January and Saint Patty's day would be a perfect time for an Irish wake, don't you think? I have always thought it is such a sad thing that the poor bloke who dies never gets to enjoy his last party."

With this somewhat unusual statement, the doctor just agreed, but told the rest our family that Dad probably would not last another week, two at most.

Obviously, the doctor did not know my father.

Dad made a list of final things he needed to get done. On the top of his list was a plan to throw his own Irish wake on Saint Patrick's Day, more than two months away. Even more startling to those who did not know him was a list of things Dad wrote on his personal calendar covering the whole year of 1984 up to Valentine's Day of 1985. The doctors humored Dad, while they planned hospice care for the end of his life, which, they were certain would be a week or two away.

Dad said he'd had enough of doctors and hospitals and decided he wanted to go home to die. The doctors agreed, so we took Dad home. He was so frail and weak, the end looked imminent.

My father set out to surprise us one and all. One day, a few days after he returned home, he disappeared when mom was shopping. Now that was no easy feat, since he was bedridden and on oxygen. But Dad had gotten up, dressed, and walked over to the funeral home to plan his own Irish wake. He expected his good friend Randy, the undertaker, to help him pull it off. My dad never let the moss grow under his feet in good times or in bad, and this situation was to be no different.

As the weeks passed, Dad seemed to grow stronger as he anticipated his goal of spending one last Saint Patrick's Day with his friends. Never mind it was to be his own wake; that thought didn't faze him at all. It seemed to give him strength and joy to check off on his calendar each task he felt the Good Lord wanted him to get done before heading home. Dad called it "Home to heaven after finishing my mission, which only me and God seem to know the ending of."

To everyone's amazement, Dad made it to Saint Patrick's Day, and his own wake, just as he had planned it. He had picked out his casket, and with the Irish humor borne through the ages, he placed it in the living room. "After all," Dad said, "an Irish wake without the coffin and the dearly departed wouldn't be an Irish wake at all." With good humor, Dad lay in the coffin as any good Irish stiff would do. There was joy and storytelling and remembering all the good times of our lives together. Our family and best friends from childhood all played up the Irish wake to the hilt, with Irish toasts and general foolishness born of the spirit of love.

Bernie, one of Dad's childhood buddies, reached over and stuck his hand in Dad's pocket. It was an old joke among friends, that whether they were rich or poor, they would trust in God's love and mercy and leave this world with empty pockets, except for their rosary.

My dad laughed and handed Bernie the rosary in his pocket, and said, "Now don't be forgetting to say the beads for me."

All in all, it was an Irish sendoff, better than any Saint Patrick's Day we had ever celebrated.

From that day on, my father remained optimistic and happy. Of course, his doctors were a bit stymied to say the least when Dad lived right up until the day he marked off the last "to do" item on his calendar.

The only item not crossed off was Valentine's Day, 1985. The day he died.

He must have even planned that. His grave marker, which he had picked out on the day he planned his own Irish Wake, was heart-shaped.

—*Christine M. Trollinger*

Chapter 6

Signs from Heaven

*Then the Lord said, "If they do not believe you
or pay attention to the first miraculous sign,
they may believe the second."*

—Exodus 4:8

57

Ten Dollars in Faith

The steps of faith fall on the seeming void,
but find the rock beneath.

—John Greenleaf Whittier

When my husband and I first met, he was not Catholic. In fact, when we began dating, he admitted that I was the first Catholic he had ever met. I was very devout in my faith, and although I never pushed my beliefs on him, I tried to lead by example. He had been raised in a lot of different churches, but the common theme in all was that the Catholic Church was just wrong.

One windy date-night we were going to the store to get a late-night snack. When we got there, he realized he had lost his last ten dollars. In college, this is equivalent to a small fortune, so we dejectedly returned to campus to search for the money. After looking in all the places we had been, I suggested he pray to St. Anthony.

He angrily shouted, "Fine! St. Anthony, if you are real, help me find my ten dollars." We got out of the car and walked across the street back to his dorm. Leaves were blowing across the road. I crossed the road first and turned when I heard an audible gasp. My husband found his ten dollars, in the middle of a busy road, on a windy fall night.

Everyday Catholicism

Needless to say, when he joined the Catholic Church three years later, St. Anthony was his patron saint. He helped us find a lot more than ten dollars that night, and I will be forever grateful.

—*Christina Robertson*

58

Bonnie's Miracle

The Lord will guide you always.

—Isaiah 58:11

Bonnie and Bob owned their own flower shop. Because of the economic conditions in the area, the availability of flowers at local grocery stores, shorter funeral viewings and Internet access, their floral business was not thriving as it had been three years earlier when they purchased it.

For about a year, my sister Bonnie and her husband Bob discussed what they should do. They debated selling. They talked about expanding into a gift shop or maybe a bookstore. But there just wasn't enough traffic or people around the area to support the business.

After reaching a point of despair one morning, Bonnie began sincerely praying and asking God for answers. Should they sell the business? Should they expand and put more money into it when it had little opportunity to survive? In desperation she prayed, "God, give me a sign telling us what You want us to do. Call me on the phone," she teased, "but show me what to do."

Soon the phone rang. A young woman was asking how much they wanted for the business. "My husband and I never take your road," she said, "but we were driving by yesterday and saw the 'For Sale' sign in the window."

Puzzled, Bonnie replied, "There isn't a sign in the window. My husband and I have been discussing whether or not we want to sell but haven't reached a decision."

"But I saw the sign!" the young lady insisted. "My husband saw it too. It was blue and white in the large picture window facing the road."

Within two weeks, the young lady and her husband bought the flower shop.

—*Kim D. Armstrong*

59

Yellow Butterfly

Why are you downcast, O my soul?
Why so disturbed within me?
Put your hope in God,
for I will yet praise him.

—Psalm 42:5

As a young girl, my biggest dream was to be a mother. I always said I wanted four children—two boys and two girls. When I got older I was so blessed to have that dream come true. I loved those kids more than life itself. Many times I found myself standing in the doorway watching as they played outside and thinking just how blessed I was, and I was always amazed that all of them were mine.

Like most mothers, in the back of my mind there was the fear that something would happen to one of them. Sadly that horror came true.

It was in June when the knock on the door came.

When my husband came to tell me the news, he didn't have to say a word. I saw into his soul that night as I looked into his eyes. Our oldest son, fourteen-year-old Josh, was hit by a car and killed.

The years after that seemed to just run together as we struggled to learn how to live life without him.

A few years later, on a beautiful spring day, my daughter Chelsea and I were going fishing. It was our favorite hobby, and we could

203

never wait until the weather got warm enough to go again. The fresh smell of newly cut grass filled the air and the daffodils were in full bloom. Everything around us seemed to be coming back to life, including us, if only for a day.

We grabbed our buckets and fishing poles and climbed over the old fence and headed down the field toward the creek. I looked back at Chelsea, who was lagging behind slightly, and saw at least thirty white butterflies dancing all around her. It was a heavenly sight, and I wondered if my Josh could communicate with us from where he was. So I called out to him several times, "Josh, if you are with us, please send us a yellow butterfly."

Then I stopped and waited as my daughter caught up with me and I told her, "If you see a yellow butterfly it means Josh is with us."

She said, "How do you know?"

"Because I asked him to send us one if he was here."

Then we both started calling out, "Josh, please send us a yellow butterfly so we'll know for sure that you are with us."

"God, please let Josh send us a yellow butterfly."

Then all of a sudden, out of nowhere a large yellow butterfly with rounded wings flew right in front of my face not three inches away! Our jaws dropped as our eyes met, and when we turned back around it was gone just as quickly as it had appeared. We couldn't see it anywhere, but we didn't need to. We had the answer we needed. With a great sense of peace we started walking toward the creek again, saying, "Come on Josh, let's go fishing!"

—*Deborah Derosier*

60

What Is Your Feather?

What strength do I have, that I should still hope?
What prospects, that I should be patient?

—Job 6:11

I turned off the kitchen faucet and cocked my head toward the sound of the television. The subject of that afternoon's talk show was "What Is Your Feather?" and I could hear the roar of applause and the host's opening monologue from my father's kitchen where I was working. Since my mother's passing earlier that year, I had been coming to this house daily after my shift in the office to cook, clean, and just generally help out my elderly dad and disabled brother, only to repeat the same process in my own home later each evening. To say that I was tired was an understatement. So I decided to leave the kitchen and sit on the edge of the living room coffee table to watch the show, and rest, just for a moment.

The guest, a middle-aged woman whose husband had died after a brief battle with cancer, went on to describe an experience that she had several months after his death. She explained that as she was walking through one of her favorite places, a park where she and her husband had shared daily strolls, she became so consumed with grief that she begged to be shown a sign of her husband's love and an indication that he continued to watch over her. The guest recounted how, as she sat on a park bench with her head in her hands, she began to sob deeply. At that moment a perfect white feather floated down from the heavens and landed softly at her feet. She had received her sign and, amazed at her answered plea, she took the feather home, framed it, and kept it in her living room as a reminder of her husband's love for her.

"Oh, how sappy," I thought. "It was just a simple coincidence. Nothing more."

The guest went on to say that she had written to the talk show host about her husband's illness and decline, her journey with grief, and her amazing feather experience. He and his staff were so moved by her story that shortly thereafter a crew was sent, courtesy of the show, to redecorate her living room around the framed item. A videotape was shown of the beautiful renovations, and the audience cheered wildly. Audience members were then asked to share their own "feather experiences," and a parade of stories began. Some participants spoke of poems, special notes, or photos all discovered post-mortem which represented a love passed, each item having its special place in their journey through grief and healing. The host then challenged all viewers to identify their own "feather" during the next commercial break.

Wearily, I rose from the spot where I sat and returned to the kitchen to continue my duties. In a moment of bitter exhaustion, I wondered why no one had yet been sent to my home to simply do a load of laundry or shop for some groceries. As I worked, I continued to consider the talk show host's challenge to define my own "feather."

My feather? I couldn't think of one. After nursing my mother through five years of what doctors called her final stages, I had no feather, just bad memories of late-night phone calls followed by rushed visits to the hospital emergency room, endless hours spent waiting in doctors' offices, and incomprehensible medical explanations. And now, with all my added responsibilities to the remaining members of my family, I didn't even have a moment to myself to breathe.

My self-pity continued to grow as I recalled how dedicated my mother and I had been to each other. We truly enjoyed each other's company and had even been on several vacations together, just the two of us. We had been closer, I surmised, than most mothers and daughters I knew. Yet, when the time came for me to move on and live my own life, she had the good grace to let me go. Even after I married, though, we remained a strong part of each other's lives. We spoke on the phone daily and often met for lunch, hunched over our burgers and fries talking girl talk. Through the years, we continued to be each other's source of strength, she helping me to stay focused during a cancer scare in my late twenties, and I helping her through her many years of illness. In those final years, she would always pat my hand before we would part. "Remember," she'd say, "no regrets when I'm gone. We had a wonderful time together here on earth."

During my drive home that evening I railed against the memories, good and bad. Didn't I, too, deserve a feather? Surely after all my mother and I had been through together, after all I had done for her, I also deserved a message of encouragement and a confirmation of love from beyond. I shook my head and tears spilled down my cheeks.

I arrived home and parked my car as I did each evening. Before exiting, I wiped my eyes and took a deep breath. Then I walked slowly down my front walkway with my head hung low. As I reached the top step I stopped, stunned. There lay one perfect white feather.

—*Monica A. Andermann*

61

Mustard Seed Angel

*If you have faith as small as a mustard seed, you can
say to this mountain, "Move from here to there," and
it will move. Nothing will be impossible to you.*

—Matthew 17:20

I never expected to be a young mother with a seriously ill child,
much less at a world-renowned pediatric and research hospital.
But then again, does any parent or child?

Like many other families there, we found immediate comfort
with the caring staff and family accommodations, which even
extended to lodging the child's healthy siblings. The hospital's mission? Discover cures and lengthen lives. Such miracles did happen
there. However, other miracles were also occurring, often unseen
by adult eyes, but thankfully claimed and witnessed through the
eyes of children.

During one of our hospital stays, I wanted to have a heart-to-
heart talk with another young mother in a similar situation. The
well siblings were away playing in a nearby staff-supervised area
while our sick children received treatments. I confided, "I could
really use some time to talk without little ears to overhear."

It was such a release to share worries and encouragement with
a kindred spirit. We soon found ourselves discussing mustard seed
faith and what Jesus had said in Scripture. "I tell you with certainty,

if you have faith like the grain of mustard seed, you can say to this mountain, 'Move from here to there,' and it will move, and nothing will be impossible to you" (Matthew 17:20).

Suddenly, my new friend's response was interrupted mid-sentence by her healthy preschool son bursting through a swinging door from the adjacent community kitchen. He grinned from ear to ear and excitedly handed his mother a small jar. He was too young to read, and we both could hardly believe the spice container labeled, "Mustard Seed."

"Matthew, where did you get this?" she asked.

"The big boy angel in the kitchen told me to give it to you."

We both stood motionless, temporarily frozen with mouths and eyes wide open in awe. My heart instantaneously warmed with indescribable joy.

Seconds later, Matthew led us to the empty room where he had seen the big boy angel, on a wall mural of handprints made by children once treated there. Chills rippled over us. Looking at all the painted handprints with each accompanying name, date, and diagnosis, we couldn't help but wonder. Could our mustard seed angel's handprints be somewhere on that wall?

Our gazes met the clock, and we realized it was, unfortunately, all too soon, time for us to resume our schedules. We talked and walked to the elevator pondering the coincidences of the angel, mustard seeds, Scripture reference from the book of Matthew, and the angelic message given to her little boy, coincidentally named Matthew.

Overwhelmed, we glanced at one another saying, "Do you really think ...?"

The empty elevator doors opened, and we could hardly believe what awaited us as we stepped inside: little, white floating feathers filled the air all around us. They tickled smiles upon our surprised faces and touched our souls with promise.

Everyday Catholicism

Feathers from an angel? Heaven only knows.

All we did know for certain was that there was only one place for our elevator and hopes to go ... "Up!"

—Patricia Morris as told to Lisa Dolensky

62

The Crucifix

You were shown these things
so that you might know that the Lord is God;
besides him there is no other.

—Deuteronomy 4:35

For centuries, reports have surfaced across the globe about divine physical signs from heaven, things like weeping marble statues of the holy Madonna or visions of Christ in the clouds above, and even manifested appearances of Mother Mary or her Son during religious holidays. The events, when authenticated, are nothing less than a modern-day miracle, and in fact, hundreds have claimed personal healings and extraordinary experiences when visiting the sites of these apparitions. As a Christian, and wanting to believe God was the mastermind behind these incredible actions and messages, I was still skeptical.

Growing up in a Christian family in Delaware, we attended church faithfully every Sunday. We professed our faith during each service with the Nicene Creed and partook in Holy Communion most weekends. Inside our home there were numerous religious artifacts around, including portraits, crucifixes in several rooms, and a stunning sculpture of Christ that hung in my parents' bedroom, a gift from my father's grandmother.

Everyday Catholicism

My brother and I shared a small bedroom growing up as boys. The wooden knotty-pine walls gave the room the feeling of a warm lakeside cabin. For most of our pubescent years, my brother and I slept in barracks-styled bunk beds. On the wall near the head of the top bunk, my bed, where I would often pray in the dark and seek the face of God after an adolescent nightmare, hung a gold-toned crucifix. Soldered to the brassy cross was the broken body of the suffering Savior, his head crowned with branches of tiny thorns, hanging in misery. It was a powerful piece and could piously sculpt your spirit. The blessed icon had been a confirmation gift when I was twelve years old. After hanging the item with a single nail through a small metal loop, we simply and sadly forgot about it. Occasionally we'd remember to dust Jesus, but generally it was a forgotten fixture.

Years later, after I graduated college and obtained an entry-level job in banking, my parents said it was time to "get your stuff." I drove to their house on a brisk autumn evening and was greeted with numerous boxes of mementos, keepsakes, photo albums, yearbooks, old toys, and junk. We spent time rummaging through the knick-knacks, cherishing each memory. Suddenly I felt old and heavy in spirit from the nostalgia. Then my brother emerged from the bedroom we once shared.

"Hey, did you want that cross hanging on the wall before you go? I'm pretty sure it was yours, not mine."

"Okay, yeah," I replied, remembering the item, and I followed him into the room.

I had grown in my faith over the years, and as a young man I had come to trust and love Jesus Christ with all my heart. Recouping this forgotten treasure and adding it to my new home was at once a devoted quest.

I reached up and removed the crucifix from the wall, holding the tarnished metal figurine in my hands, gently and with great respect. The symbol of the cross had become the heart of my faith, and I turned most reverent anytime I viewed one. I felt the smoothness and the contrasting jaggedness of the crucifix across my palm and brooded over the agonizing pain and misery the Son of God suffered on my behalf. It made me shudder.

Then I noticed something else that made me shudder.

In the specific area where the crucifix had been hanging, there was a long, flowing stain on the pinewood. It was a dark black cherry color with a lacquered look. It glistened slightly as if wet and fresh. It resembled blood.

I touched the stain, which ran nearly to the flooring panel. It was part of the wood, and its prominence stood out suddenly as if under a spotlight. A speedy but thorough survey of the room showed no other panels even closely resembling this one. The bleeding stain was unique to this single panel of wood.

Puzzled, I replaced the crucifix on the wall, searching for a logical explanation. There had to be one. Perhaps, I reasoned, the screw that was used to hang the crucifix had somehow caused a fissure in the wood, which led ultimately to this meandering stain.

But the single tributary started exactly where Christ's nail-pierced hand laid against the cross beam, several inches away from the small screw hole.

The episode spooked me initially, but then my mood changed. I was overcome with emotion, looking down at the grief-stricken face of my tortured Savior, then at the shed blood stained into the bedroom wall. I found myself rubbing my fingers deferentially across the stain as tears brimmed my eyes.

My brother confirmed, "It's a miracle." My parents agreed.

Years later, the stain remains, a permanent fixture on the panel of pine. I still have the crucifix in my home and on occasion have taken it over to my parents' house to again verify the miracle.

Everyday Catholicism

And now I am a believer. I believe He communicates with us in supernatural modes, through crying statues, or visions of Christ in the clouds above, and yes, even in simple crucifixes hung on a young boy's wall.

—*David Michael Smith*

63

The Carpenter's Son

That night God appeared to Solomon and said to him,
"Ask for whatever you want me to give you."

—2 Chronicles 1:7

A life built around a full-time job, three children, and a husband who worked the midnight shift was wearing me down. There had to be more to my life than paperwork, potty training, and ridiculous factory schedules. And then there was that nagging thought that kept tugging at my skirt like a whiny child: "There's something else you should be doing." It refused to stop begging for attention.

When I read the announcement in my church bulletin, I knew it was just what I needed: a retreat. Maybe there God could answer the restlessness in me.

The weekend retreat was to be held in a convent. I had never been to one. Walking onto the grounds, I passed towering brick buildings that stood like soldiers guarding holy ground. Standing regally in the center of the compound was an elderly oak tree. Years of rain, like holy water, had blessed it with a long life. Its massive bouquet of branches reached for the sky like hands lifted in charismatic prayer. I stopped for a moment under their gesture of praise, letting the holiness of this place enfold me.

Later, having navigated to my room, I lay my suitcase on the bed and surveyed my surroundings. The room was stark and simple: a bed, desk, Bible, and dresser. A crucifix hung on the gray wall.

"Things look pretty bleak around here," I thought. Peace may have escorted me in, but I wondered if simplicity and I would be good roommates.

That night I crawled into bed and cocooned myself in blankets, trying to make myself cozy. Silence crept around the drab space. The quiet made me uncomfortable. But, in spite of my uneasiness, exhaustion tucked me in and I quickly fell asleep.

I don't know how long I had been slumbering when my eyes sprang open. I gasped, then yelled. Looming before me was a goliath ghostly figure of a boy standing as tall as the ceiling! A thin band circled his head like a leather halo, holding his long, curly hair away from his face. His body was wet with sweat. His head tilted upward with an affectionate gaze aimed toward heaven.

In the second it took to open my eyes, I was infused with knowledge, a holy résumé introducing my spiritual intruder: "This is Jesus, the Carpenter's Son. He has been working long grueling hours helping his father build."

And then I heard the words, not audibly, but inside me. "It's hard work building the Kingdom."

I sat upright in the bed and speedily brushed my hand over the figure like I was erasing a chalkboard. And, just like that, He was gone.

Bewildered, I lay back down and tried to assimilate what had just happened. I stared at the dull gray wall that had been the backdrop of this mysterious visitation. My heart pounded like a hammer. "If that was Jesus, then why am I so afraid?"

The answer came to me in the memory of a Bible passage I had read. The disciples were on a boat in the middle of a storm when Jesus headed their way, walking on the water. At first they didn't recognize him. "It's a ghost!" they screamed out in fear.

I knew just how those guys felt. I was terrified. Evidently, holy fear is a very scary thing. But, the revelation that Jesus had scared the devil out of his disciples, too, comforted me. The consoling thought wrapped its arms around me, calming my fear until I drifted back to sleep.

The next morning was Sunday. I went to Mass with the previous night's encounter on my mind. As Mass started, I was distracted by my thoughts, but praying nonetheless. "Lord, was that really you last night?"

When the time came for the priest to deliver the homily, he paced slowly at the front of the church. Stroking both sides of his chin, as if engrossed in deep thought, he said, reverently, "Jesus the Carpenter's Son. What a beautiful name for Jesus."

I was stunned.

"This is no coincidence," I told myself. "God is definitely trying to tell me something!"

I felt like someone had plugged me in; electric currents surged up and down my body. I was vibrating. Goose bumps sprung up all over me. The phenomenon reoccurred in waves throughout the sermon and did not stop until Mass ended.

Thoughts of Jesus traveled with me on the long drive home. Trying to understand why He would appear to me as the Carpenter's Son, I asked myself questions: "What does a carpenter do?" He builds things. "What does Jesus, the Carpenter, do?" He builds lives.

As soon as I got home, I sat down at my computer and wrote about Jesus, the Carpenter's Son, the builder of lives. On a whim, I submitted what I had written to the editor of my diocesan newspaper. To my surprise, he invited me to write a monthly column for the newspaper. I heard the Call. I started writing.

A short time later, I was asked to be a cantor and music minister at my church. Again, I heard the Call. I started singing.

Everyday Catholicism

One thing led to another, and suddenly, I had plenty to do. Seems there's a lot of heavenly work out there. The floodgates opened, and I just went with the flow.

My visit from the Carpenter's Son was over twenty years ago. Not one day since then have I been idle; I always find something worthwhile to do for Jesus. Like writing, singing, visiting nursing homes, or teaching catechism to my grandchildren. Often, I get tired. Sometimes I want to quit. But, for the most part, when weariness comes a-calling, I just take a break. Then, I look to heaven and wipe the sweat from my brow, remembering that Jesus once told me that it's hard work building the Kingdom of God.

—*Teresa Anne Hayden*

64

Angel in the Snow

See, I am sending an angel ahead of you
to guard you along the way and to bring you
to the place I have prepared.

—Exodus 23:20

I felt the vibration of my cell phone hiding in my pocket. I could barely hear through the screaming. "It's amazing and yet so mysterious! I don't know how it got there!"

"What got there, Kathy? What are you talking about?"

"The angel! There's a drawing of an angel in the snow outside Kelly's bedroom window! It's blowing a horn and has a flowing robe. It looks like a child drew it with a stick or something. It's smack in the middle of the big hill in our backyard. But how did it get there? There are no tracks around it!"

Later that afternoon, my minivan made its way up the familiar mountain to visit my friend. I explained to my two sons the reason for this trip. They were used to going with me to visit Kathy and her little girl Kelly, who had terminal brain cancer. She'd fought a tremendous battle and was now only days away from leaving the earth.

She'd had a miracle already. Her brain stem had ruptured, leaving her in a vegetative state. The doctors had proclaimed her clinically brain dead and took her off life support. A few hours later, she awoke and looked at her father and said, "Daddy, paint, hotdog."

Now Kelly was back home and the family was waiting. It had been two weeks since her big miracle and now her days were numbered. We all were praying.

The boys and I got out of our car into the freezing cold winds of February. Kathy met us and walked us out back. My sons had difficulty tromping in the deep snow. But soon they shouted, "Mommy, Mommy, I see the angel! There it is!"

My mouth hung open wide. In the middle of this massive snow-covered hill was a drawing of an enormous angel, seemingly drawn by a child. There was not a track or flaw in the snow around it.

Two weeks later, on Valentine's Day, with the setting sun and a brilliant red sky, little Kelly passed on. Likely, the heralding snow angel escorted her home.

—*Marisa A. Snyder*

65

The Little Lamb

He tends his flock like a shepherd;
he gathers the lambs in his arms
and carries them close to his heart.

—Isaiah 40:11

"God, I really need You today," I whispered, grabbing a handful of
sand and watching the grains flow from my closed fist. "Here I am,
feeling like that little lost lamb again."

I loved this image of myself as a lamb being protected by the
Good Shepherd. It helped me feel free to talk to God. As a single
mother, I prayed for each of my four children and for the ability
to take care of them. It was overwhelming keeping my family out
of trouble, and at times I feared that I was failing miserably. Some
days, like this, brought feelings of being alone and abandoned.

That morning, while reading the Bible I came across the verse,
"He will feed His flock like a shepherd; He will gather the lambs in
His arm" (Isaiah 40:11). This Scripture had a special meaning to
me. It had been shown to me a few months earlier by a counselor,
when I'd approached her for prayer because of a hard situation
I was having with my daughter. The counselor, underlining the
words with her finger, had emphasized the remaining text, "He will
carry them in His bosom and will gently lead those with young."
I took this as a promise from God that He was there to help me

raise my children, providing the grace I needed. Although it was encouraging to be reminded of this again, my sadness lingered. I needed something more.

It was warm and sunny, so on my way home from work I decided to go to the beach. I drove to State Beach, a stretch of shoreline over four miles long. Since it was September, off-season, the beach was deserted. I could choose anywhere along the road to stop. I arbitrarily picked a spot, parked my car, and trudged over the dune and down a path. As I sat on my towel, my gaze searched the untroubled sea and cloudless sky.

Picking up a seashell, I started dragging it along the sand in a wide arc about me. "Father God," I murmured, recalling a verse from the psalms, "Your thoughts to me are precious and ... they're more in number than the sand." I swallowed hard. "I need You."

As the shell in my hand dug into the sand, it struck something hard. I glimpsed a bit of white. Sweeping away the sand with my fingers, a little plastic figure emerged. I picked it up. When I realized what it was, a shock of surprise and joy hit me.

Had some child brought his toy farm animals to the beach last summer, leaving this behind? And if so, what were the odds that out of four miles of beach I picked this dune to walk down and this spot on which to sit?

Or had a loving Creator planted it, a special gift, in the sand where I sat?

For in my hand was the figure of a lamb, a message from God to me.

—*Donna Paulson*

66

Fishing for Rainbow Trout

We live in a rainbow of chaos.

—Paul Cézanne

Okay, so maybe it was a little irresponsible for my dad to embark on a fishing trip and leave his pregnant wife alone at home. My mother was seven months swollen with twins. Other, more rational couples might've promised to stay side-by-side, but we babies weren't due until August, and this fishing trip was a graduation present for my brother. Before the little girl duo was to come into the world, the two males of the family needed to bond in the manliest way they knew—fishing for rainbow trout.

So my dad bade goodbye to my very pregnant mother and set off for Oregon with my older brother. Perhaps Dad was oblivious to the foreshadowing of sudden rain and hot whistling winds, finding satisfaction in the masculine angst of raging seething rivers. Either way, it must have come as a shock to return to his lodge one evening and receive ten frantic messages left by my mother. It's hard to guess exactly what she babbled, for a hysterical woman in labor is not usually known for her eloquence, but my dad knew instantly he had to get home. He and my brother leapt into the car and rocketed down the road, racing off in less than five minutes for the fifteen-hour car ride to San Francisco.

Everyday Catholicism

Meanwhile, my mother felt her babies' impatience and rushed to her car. She was so enormous she couldn't even buckle her seatbelt, and her stomach constantly set off the horn. Our neighbor had agreed to drive my mother to the hospital in case my dad was unavailable, but Mom chose not to trouble her backup chauffeur and instead drove herself.

Meanwhile, my father and brother sped down the highway. Despite all efforts to surpass the speed limits as quietly and cautiously as possible, Dad was pulled over by a cop just as my mother teetered into the hospital. My parents' despair was mutual as Dad pleaded with an unsympathetic policeman and my mother hid in the elevator, embarrassed by her frazzled state.

At last, speeding ticket begrudgingly accepted, my dad was on the road again just as my mother leaned over and grasped the nurse's desk, mumbling, "I think something's wrong."

The nurse was a warm and no-nonsense woman. If her husband had asked to go on a fishing trip seven months into her pregnancy, she would have said, "You think some darn fish are more important than staying home and rubbing my feet? I don't have cravings for trout; I need chocolate ice cream!" The nurse told my mother to remove her pants and with one mighty sniff declared, "Honey, this ain't no false alarm. Your water broke!"

At the same time, massive rain clouds broke over Northern California, and a sudden downpour impaired my dad's speeding. This was enough to discourage anyone, for despite the near-slapstick calamity of our impromptu births, this premature labor was serious. There'd been another of us, my unknown brother, but our trio was reduced by a miscarriage before he even had a name.

As Dad's car flew through the rain, however, we decided we'd been patient long enough. My mother begged for painkillers. My father must have sensed her despair and agony. He sensed that he would never get to San Francisco in time for our births. Though the rain slowly let up, he knew he could never drive fast enough to make it ... assuming we made it too. He was frightened and discouraged and tired. Just as his weary mind considered the worst possible scenario, he looked out the window and saw a glimmer on the horizon.

Across the sky stretched a double rainbow. Not one, but two radiant arcs, one on top of the other. My father stared long and hard at this double rainbow, two for his double dose of Gemini girls. He knew just by looking at that pair of rainbows that everything would be all right. This was a sign, and with hope restored he continued down the road, slowing his frantic speed to gaze at those rainbows a little longer.

He arrived at the hospital seven hours after we were born. Two months premature, I weighed three pounds, fifteen ounces; McKenzie was four pounds, three ounces. Though the double rainbow calmed my father, he was still terribly on edge until he saw us, our tiny wrinkled bodies warming under the orange glow of incubator lights. When Dad arrived, Mom awoke to hold us, and we smiled, brown eyes all around, except for my mother's glistening wet violet ones.

Dad's fishing trip had been cut short, but he didn't mind. All he needed at that moment was the tenderness only two baby girls could give.

After that day, Dad never saw another double rainbow.

—*Brittany Newell, age 16*

67

Balloons of Hope

In your unfailing love you will lead the people you have redeemed.
In your strength you will guide them to your holy dwelling.

—Exodus 15:13

"Okay. One, two, three, let them go!" I shouted. Sue's three young children, Stephanie, Kristen, and Billy, released the purple balloons covered with messages of love.

It was a cold March afternoon. A misty rain fell as we stood in Sue's driveway to mark the second anniversary of her passing. The dismal weather reflected how I felt in my heart, but I mustered up a smile for the children's sake. My twin sister Sue, just forty-one years old, had died suddenly, leaving behind her children and her husband Bill.

Just yesterday, while chatting with my friend, I mentioned Sue's upcoming anniversary. Mary, who knew firsthand the heartache of loss after the passing of her ten-year-old son John, offered me an idea.

"For John's birthday we write messages to him on balloons. Then we release them."

I headed for the store and bought three purple balloons, since purple was Sue's favorite color.

Now here I stood watching the balloons leave the little hands that held them so tightly. Privately, before liftoff, I read many of the messages. They tugged at my heart. *I miss you, Mommy. To my loving wife, all my love. We love you Aunt Suzy.* And the one I added, using her nickname: *I miss you Twinpop!*

Filled with anticipation, we watched as the balloons were released. Immediately, they drifted down onto the driveway. It was too cold. Realizing my mistake, I thought I should have waited for a nicer day. I prayed, "Please, God, help us!"

Suddenly, the wind kicked up. I held my breath as the balloons slowly lifted. Two floated up past the trees to the sky, but the third wedged itself between two branches. "Uh oh," Sue's youngest, Billy, exclaimed. "It's going to pop!" Sue's husband, Bill, and I looked at each other.

"Oh boy," he whispered. Again I prayed, "Please, God, don't let them pop!"

The kids began to cheer for the one lone purple balloon. Slowly, it began to creep out of its trap, bobbing along the prickly branches until it made its way to freedom. "Go! Go! Go!" the kids shouted. We let out a collective sigh as we watched the balloon finally edge its way around the trees, miraculously not popping. It then took off to catch up with the other two and sailed out of sight. "Thank you God," I offered silently. I looked around at all the smiles, and I knew somewhere in heaven, Sue was smiling too.

A week later, my youngest, Caroline, was upstairs. She looked out her bedroom window, then called to me, "Mommy, there is a purple balloon out back. Is it the one we sent Aunt Suzy?"

I glanced out the kitchen window and spotted a purple balloon bouncing on the grass. I walked out the back door to take a closer look. As I approached, the balloon took off through my neighbor's yard, with me in my pajamas chasing after it. Finally, I grabbed the purple balloon. It looked identical to the ones we sent, minus the messages. Hmm. What a coincidence. I brought the balloon into our house. Caroline asked, "Mommy, did Aunt Suzy send you that balloon?"

"I wouldn't doubt it, Caroline," I answered with a smile.

Everyday Catholicism

That same spring my mom became very sick. After a series of mini strokes, she was weak and confused and could no longer live alone. She soon developed dementia. I prayed daily as I placed Mom's name on several nursing home waiting lists. I knew they could care for her in a way I could not physically do.

Months passed and my mom continued to decline. It had been a frustrating afternoon of phone calls to nursing homes, agencies, and family. After one particular phone call ended with an abrupt "no," tears filled my eyes. I was exhausted. Between dealing with the loss of my twin sister and now the concern I felt for my mom, I was overwhelmed emotionally, physically, and spiritually. Wiping away my tears, I grabbed my coat and called to my kids, "I am going for a walk."

It had started to snow. As I walked, the snowflakes mingled with my tears. I talked to my sister and prayed to God. "Please God, help me! Sue, what am I going to do?" I thought about the past two years and wondered how much more I could handle. Where would I get the strength to continue?

As I turned the corner, I noticed the snow and wind beginning to pick up. But it was not all I noticed. On my neighbor's front lawn, one purple balloon gently bobbed up and down in the snow. I could not believe it. My heart lifted. The purple balloon again. I knew the days ahead would be tough, but I was encouraged knowing I was not handling this alone.

On Christmas morning, my mom had a seizure and was admitted to the hospital. Ten days later, she was stabilized and scheduled for discharge. She was now blind in one eye and could no longer feed herself or walk. In addition, she was confused most of the time. Mom needed round-the-clock care. The hospital found a temporary placement for her fifteen miles away. After she was admitted, I gradually realized it was a terrible nursing home.

Once I found her asleep with her face lying in a full plate of food. She often looked disheveled, unclean, and isolated. At first

I thought, "Maybe they are just understaffed today. Or perhaps the staff is still getting her into a routine." But soon it became clear I had to get her out of that place.

I was filled with guilt; I could not physically care for her myself. At this point I couldn't even lift her. I begged God, "Please find her another place. Sue, watch over her." Then I began my futile search for a new nursing home.

On my birthday, I drove over to see my mom. I thought back to happier days and all the celebrations my mom, Sue, and I had shared on this special day. Turning into the parking lot, my joyful birthday memories were soon clouded with concern for Mom.

Saddened, I entered her room. There underneath her shabby metal-framed bed, was a purple balloon. I was stunned! "Mom, where did you get that purple balloon?" I asked in astonishment.

"I don't know," she answered. "Someone gave it to me this morning." I smiled.

A few weeks later, at work, my boss asked, "How are things with your mom?"

"Not good," I responded. "She is still on waiting lists for a better nursing home."

"My grandmother lived at Pembrooke for years. It was great!" a coworker chimed in.

I had never heard of Pembrooke, but I made a call. Miraculously a room was available.

My mom was being transferred by ambulance. I planned to be there when she arrived. Driving up the pike, I was so nervous. "Is this a nice place, Lord?" I kept watch for the new nursing home. But it was easy to spot.

Tied to the post just across from the Pembrooke sign was one lone purple balloon.

—*Donna Teti*

68

Beads

Prayer is as much the instinct of my nature as a Christian
as it is a duty enjoined by the command of God.

—Tryon Edwards

It was not the usual party talk.

"I know it sounds weird," confided my friend, Josie, between bites of brie. "But I've started saying the rosary again."

Josie is a thoroughly modern woman. She has a career, a husband, and three sons. She works hard to keep everything balanced, including the family's meals and her own checkbook.

When she told me about reconnecting with this ancient Catholic ritual, she lowered her voice and looked around to make sure no one would overhear. I think Josie considered her statement shockingly retrograde for a Southern California woman at the start of the millennium.

Her admission brought back my own Catholic girlhood. Through that tangle of early memories winds a long string of rosaries: fancy First Communion rosaries with mother-of-pearl crucifixes and clattering cut-glass beads, lightweight glow-in-the-dark rosaries, tinged creamy yellow by day, shining ghostly green on my dresser in the dark of night. There were rosaries I made myself in youthful bursts of Catholic craftsmanship.

Beads

In summers, before the Sixties' heyday of macramé, my grade-school friends and I spent many August afternoons knotting thin waxy cord into misshapen beads. Not that we were particularly religious. Making rosaries was a time-passing crafts project, something we did when it was too hot to roller skate. We'd lounge on collapsible lawn chairs near our mothers' rose bushes, talking about the boys in our class we liked and the girls we didn't. And when we weren't reaching for the Kool-Aid, we twisted twine. We had a certain-sized knot for Hail Marys. A larger one for Our Fathers and Glory Bes. And the most complicated of all for the Apostles' Creed, the lengthy prayer that got the whole thing rolling. Sometimes we'd save these creations to give to our grandmothers. More often, we'd drop them at afternoon's end into the kitchen's catch-all drawer, the one with all the ballpoint pens that didn't work.

Every funeral I ever went to when I was young featured a rosary resting in the deceased's eternal grasp. These were serious, grown-up rosaries. Usually black, with smooth, oblong beads linked by shiny bits of silver chain.

I remember rosaries as a kind of fashion accessory for the nuns who taught us, their woolen habits loosely cinched by a weighty strand of wooden beads. And a rosary was as much a part of my grandmother's hands as the age spots.

Rosaries were part of everyday life, like tuna sandwiches on Fridays and Ed Sullivan on Sundays. And saying the rosary was as natural to me then as outgrowing last year's saddle shoes.

Those days are gone. Not just for me, but for many Catholics everywhere. In less than one generation, a centuries-old tradition all but vanished, disappearing like a puff of incense in a cavernous cathedral. Choirs began singing "Kumbaya" instead of intoning Gregorian chants. In place of an old religion's incalculable mysteries, came something called "relevance." And fingering beads, while muttering more than fifty Hail Marys, seemed about as relevant as Sunday services in the language of Julius Caesar.

Many of the changes brought a much-needed breath of fresh air to an institution in danger of terminal mustiness. But the winds of change that coursed through those opened stained-glass windows blew a lot of people's rosary beads into a forgotten corner, mine included, along with Josie's.

And there they stayed. Through decades of anti-war protests and rising divorce rates, assassinations and a growing drug culture. Through the Cold War and free love, terrorists attacks and an AIDS epidemic. Into an era of race riots, drive-by shootings, and white-collar fraud. In a society that makes Madonna rich and too often leaves its homeless hungry. In a country where a gruesome double murder trial was televised daily on the Entertainment Channel.

A faithless time, when you think about it. And Josie did, as she shook the dust from her rosary beads. She says she now finds praying the rosary meditative, almost mantra-like, and infinitely soothing to her soul. Peggy Noonan, a former speechwriter for the first President Bush, says the same thing in her book, *Life, Liberty, and the Pursuit of Happiness*. She admits that lunch hours today sometimes find her at church, kneeling with the old ones who through the years never put down their beads.

I know that two examples do not make a movement. But something seems to be going on here. Maybe we're slowly realizing that a custom hundreds of years old offers a permanence that we lost in the Age of Information. Could be that our grandmothers—and their grandmothers before them—were onto something. I'm beginning to see again that there's something to be said for a simple faith, a faith that embraces mysteries, a faith unafraid to offer awe instead of answers.

Beads

In a world spinning into the first decades of the twenty-first century, it's comforting to know there are still a few rosaries around to hold onto.

—*Sue Diaz*

69

Sacraments Make Me Hungry

Jesus Christ, the condescension of divinity
and the exaltation of humanity.

—Phillips Brooks

It was an evening wedding during the Christmas season, elegant with poinsettias, hurricane lamps, red velvet dresses, and boutonnieres. The string quartet played Purcell's stirring *Trumpet Voluntary* for the entrance procession. As the bride and groom, shaking with joy and fear, said their vows to one another, so full of gratitude for this wondrous love, I turned to my husband, Ben, and said, "I'm hungry."

He rolled his eyes. "You're always hungry at weddings."

I had to admit he was right.

The truth is, give me a bride and groom, a room full of love and hearts full of hope and I start hungering for champagne and wedding cake.

A wet and squirmy baby, newly baptized and held up to the adoring congregation, makes me think of cookies and punch and bowls of salty cashews.

I remember everything I had to eat at all the sacraments of my childhood. My baby brother's baptism party, held in our garage, had platters of Sloppy Joes and corned beef sandwiches, icy bottles of beer and pop, chips and dips and—oh, blessed of childhood memories—homemade ice cream and chocolate cake. Now that's a baptism!

Sacraments Make Me Hungry

Confirmation was spaghetti and meatballs, garlic bread and salad, brownies and ice cream, and special Shirley Temples for the new soldiers in Christ.

But the most indelible memory is the reception our parents gave us after our First Communions. At Mass, the girls all had crisp, crinkly white dresses and the boys wore white or black suits. We carried our white missals or our tiny colored rosaries up to the altar, where we knelt on soft leather as the priest placed the host on our tongues. We returned to our pews and placed our heads in our hands, doing our best to imitate the piety of our parents. And then afterward, Sister Vivian led us into the school cafeteria, now transformed with balloons and beautiful tablecloths. There were little paper cups of mints and nuts at each place, plates of pancakes and scrambled eggs, tiny glasses of orange juice, and even cups of hot chocolate.

Ben nudged me from my caloric reverie, and I watched as the bride and groom received Communion.

Suddenly I knew.

"I know why I am always hungry at weddings," I whispered to Ben. "Because the Eucharist, the mother of all sacraments, relies on food to bring us God. Food. Real bread. Real wine. Real Jesus." *For my flesh is true food and my blood is true drink* (John 6:55).

I knew it that day I walked into the transformed cafeteria, with beaming parents and sweet pancakes. I've known it after every sacramental celebration, with its punch and cookies and buffet tables and sit-down dinners.

It's all about food ... real food that sustains real people, hungry for a relationship with the Real Jesus.

No wonder sacraments make me hungry. They're supposed to.

—*Kathy McGovern*

70

A Eucharistic Experience

Come to me all you who labor and are
burdened and I will give you rest.

—Matthew 11:28

It was December 24, 1961, midnight Mass, one of the most joyous celebrations in the liturgical calendar. Why was I trying to convince myself that I should remain in the choir loft at Communion and deprive myself of the precious Body and Blood of Jesus Christ? My misery and pain were standing in the way of my wanting to go to Communion.

Following a routine bone graft, there had been months of frequent surgeries and long hospital stays, leaving me with uncontrollable infections in the wound. The end of treatment came on the day my doctor said the words no one wants to hear, "I cannot do anything else to help you. You'll just have to live with it."

"It" was a swollen, angry red foot that had a three-inch round hole eroded in the side and a frozen ankle that did not bend at all. This created a deep limp resembling a pumping motion when I walked. I could not stand to wear a regular shoe, so I wore a canvas tennis shoe split all the way down to the rubber toe to allow room for the swelling. The worst of it all was being in pain all day, every day, and sometimes throughout the night.

A Eucharistic Experience

The hospital and doctor bills had financially devastated us, and there was no money to buy more than one pair of canvas shoes, so the pair I wore was slightly soiled. Definitely there was no money to buy festive holiday clothing to wear to the midnight Mass.

My return to our church choir, following my extended illness, had been an effort as I tried to rekindle my connection with God and with my church. My faith had become shaky due to pain, disappointment, worry, and having my whole life turned upside down. I felt God had all but abandoned me. I had gone to confession to prepare for the holiday season and was determined to participate, as I always had in the past. I had attended all the choir rehearsals and I was ready, or so I thought.

Christmas Eve arrived and, as always, the church was filled to capacity, and then some. As I entered the church, the smell of incense filled the air, combined with perfumes belonging to the many ladies wearing their beautiful furs, hats, and holiday best.

Although the stairs were a struggle, I welcomed the chance to disappear to the choir loft where I couldn't be seen by the congregation. I wore my gray and blue plaid wool skirt and a light blue sweater. These were the best I had and, of course, my feet were clad in my slightly soiled, slit to the toe, canvas tennis shoes. But it really didn't matter; no one would see me.

We sang the half-hour Christmas program we had been rehearsing for the past few weeks, and the lovely joyous music penetrated my very being. I was caught up in the celebration and feeling very good when the Mass began. As we progressed toward the Communion part of the Mass, my stomach began to feel queasy and my heart was beating faster. Panic was setting in and clouding my concentration. I could not bear the thought of limping pitifully all the way down the center aisle to the Communion rail wearing my plain clothes and split tennis shoe. I quickly decided I would just stay in the choir loft and let everyone else go without me. I would be safe. I started to feel a little less nauseated.

Suddenly, another feeling surged over me — a longing so great I could not ignore it. I desperately wanted to receive the Eucharist. I needed to receive the Eucharist. The internal struggle was overwhelming, my fear of being stared at and pitied battling with my desire to receive the Body and Blood of Jesus Christ. I was singing, but my mind was whirling out of control. Then, I heard myself saying the words aloud, "Lord, I am not worthy to receive you, but only say the word and I shall be healed."

It was time to go to Communion.

I sat frozen for an instant. All at once, I stood, started toward the stairs, down the center aisle, and toward the Communion rail. I walked, looking down at the floor and wishing I could vanish upward like the smoke from the incense. I fought back tears. I could feel heads turn and stares falling on me, like arrows from an archer's bow, as I limped down the aisle to where Father was distributing the Host. I looked up as he said, "Body of Christ." My response, "Amen," was loud and clear. Suddenly, I felt a warm feeling spreading over my whole being as I turned to go back to the choir loft. I suddenly felt different. I felt wonderful. I felt joy.

My journey back up the center aisle was not the same as it was coming down. I was still dressed the same, my gait was the same pumping motion, but this time my head was held high and I looked into the eyes of the people kneeling along the aisle as I walked. I felt great inside and out. The pain was lessened by this new feeling of peace and joy deep inside.

My life changed dramatically that night. I was no longer plagued by worry about what I wore or how I walked, nor did I let the relentless pain keep my mind from seeing what was really important in my life. God made me realize that my suffering wasn't from being poor or physically afflicted, but from my foolish pride and my own self-pity. God took away my feelings of sorrow and misery and gave me a renewed spirit to bear up under my hardships and go on living my life in a more spiritual way.

The Blessed Infant truly gave me a wonderful and lasting gift. The joy and true meaning of Christmas had settled in my soul and, from that night on, it was there to stay.

—Joyce Sudbeck

Meet Our Contributors!

Note: These bios were current as of 2010.

Diana M. Amadeo has been married to Len for thirty-four years. They have three children and three grandchildren. Besides writing books, articles, and stories, Diana enjoys her Beagle, indulges in travel, and reaps the harvest of her greenhouse. This is her seventh publication in the *Chicken Soup for the Soul* series. Contact her at DA.author@comcast.net.

Monica A. Andermann is a writer who lives on Long Island with her husband/proofreader, Bill, and their cat, Charley. Her work has been widely published both online and in print, including several credits in *Chicken Soup for the Soul* and *A Cup of Comfort* collections.

Kim D. Armstrong has been a registered nurse for thirty years. She has published two books of stories about the miraculous healing of patients who were given a death sentence. Kim lives in western Pennsylvania with her husband, teenage daughter and son. E-mail her at kimdarlenearmstrong@embarqmail.com or check out her website: www.kimarmstrong.net.

Pam Durant Aubry is a freelance writer, mommy, and former plus-sized model. She is a graduate of Temple University and has a Bachelor of Arts degree in journalism. Pam is also a Microsoft

Certified Trainer and teaches classes at a computer training school. She is working on her first novel. E-mail her at pameladurant@comcast.net.

Cynthia Bilyk is currently working on her bachelors in psychology. She recently quit her job and became a stay-at-home mom. She enjoys reading, the outdoors, and volunteer work. Please e-mail her at ufodonkey@gmail.com.

Pam Bostwick's many articles appear in Christian magazines, newspapers, and anthologies, including several in *Chicken Soup for the Soul*. Although visually and hearing impaired, she enjoys her country home, loves the beach, plays guitar, and is a volunteer counselor. She has seven children and eleven grandchildren and is happily remarried. E-mail her at pamloves7@verizon.net.

Theresa Chan is an entrepreneur, world traveler, and published author from Toronto, Ontario. This is her second story appearing in the *Chicken Soup for the Soul* series, the first appearing in *Chicken Soup for the Bride's Soul*. Her story is a tribute to all the angels in her life. Contact her via e-mail at tccsheba@yahoo.ca.

Jeri Chrysong resides in Huntington Beach, California, where you will often find her walking her Pug Mabel. Jeri loves being a grandma to Lucas and Clay. She enjoys Hawai'i and photography. Her writing's current focus is her weight loss journey into wellness. Visit Jeri's weight loss blog at http://jchrysong.wordpress.com.

Joan Clayton is a retired teacher. Joan was the "Woman of the Year" in 2003 in her town and has been twice in *Who's Who Among America's Teachers*. Joan is the religion columnist for her town's local newspaper. Visit her website at www.joanclayton.com.

Leesa Culp resides outside of Niagara Falls, Ontario, along with her husband and two children. Leesa enjoys writing, running, hockey, and spending time with her family. She is currently working on her first non-fiction book about a Western Canadian hockey team. She can be reached via e-mail at leesadculp@yahoo.ca.

Diana DeAndrea-Kohn is the owner of a small business. She is married to her husband, Scott. She has three boys: Kenny, Alex, and Brodie. She spends her free time reading and writing.

Deborah Derosier is the mother of four and Memaw of two. She enjoys fishing, scrapbooking, and writing poetry.

Sue Diaz is an author, writing teacher, and essayist whose work has appeared in numerous regional and national publications, including *Newsweek, Family Circle, Woman's Day, Christian Science Monitor,* and *Reader's Digest.* Her website—www.suediaz.com—tells all. You can contact her at sue@suediaz.com.

Shirley Dino lives in Denver, Colorado, with her husband, Sandy. She is a lector at her parish and enjoys tennis, biking, and gardening. In addition to her three sons and two wonderful daughter-in-laws, she has three grandchildren.

Melissa Dykman is a happily married twenty-seven-year-old mother of one. She has been blessed with a wonderful family. God has been good to her.

Delores Fraga-Carvalho has been married to Luis for 33 years and is mother to Lisa-Marie, 31, and Luis, Jr., 25. She is a member of The Red Hat Society local chapters in Moses Lake, Washington, Rebel Reds and Desert Reds. She crochets and enjoys water aerobics. Please e-mail her at divinedamedee@accima.com.

Ellen C. K. Giangiordano graduated from Temple University School of Law in 1990 and was a litigator for eight years in Philadelphia before returning home to raise her five children. Ellen enjoys cooking, sewing, weight lifting, yoga, spending time with her family, and reading the works of John Paul II. Ellen and her family now live in Georgia.

Gene Giggleman received his Doctor of Veterinary Medicine degree from Texas A&M University in 1981. He is a full-time college administrator, teaches human anatomy, and has a small animal veterinary practice. He enjoys reading, riding motorcycles and bicycles, fishing, gardening, being outdoors, and spending time with his grandchildren.

Terry Gniffke is active in his church, CEO of Caliber Media Group, Inc., and co-founder of Websites for Heroes. Terry and his wife have three grown children. Darlene Palermo's father and uncle were itinerant evangelists who travelled the world for sixty years. Their stories are her heritage.

Rosemary Goodwin was born in the lovely country town, Bury St. Edmunds in Suffolk County, England. You can see her hometown on her website: www.Rosemary-Goodwin.com. After moving to the U.S. with her military husband, Rosemary lived in New England and currently lives in a historic town in Eastern Pennsylvania.

Judy Lee Green is an award-winning writer and speaker whose spirit and roots reach deep into the Appalachian Mountains. Tennessee-bred and cornbread-fed, she has been published hundreds of times and received dozens of awards for her work. Her family is the source for many of her stories. She lives in Tennessee. Reach her at JudyLeeGreen@bellsouth.net.

Heidi H. Grosch (www.heidigrosch.com) is an international writer and educator who daily celebrates the miracle of learning. She works in the Norwegian school system, writes for the *Norwegian American Weekly* (www.norway.com), and is developing a new website focused on English as a global language (www.childrenslit-eraturenetwork.org).

Elaine Hanson lives in Fort Collins, Colorado, near Vaughn and his family. After telling the story in a Bible class, she was delighted when Linda L. Osmundson wanted to write it for a *Chicken Soup for the Soul* book. Linda's stories have appeared in eight *Chicken Soup for the Soul* books as well as over sixty other publications.

Mandy Hastings is the pen name of Jennie Ivey, who lives in Tennessee. She is a newspaper columnist and the author of three books. She has published numerous fiction and non-fiction pieces, including stories in several *Chicken Soup for the Soul* books. Contact her at jivey@frontiernet.net.

Teresa Anne Hayden is a writer who lives in Cayce, Kentucky, with her husband Mike. They have three children and six grandchildren. Her work has appeared in *Catholic Digest*, the *Rural Kentuckian*, and *The Western Kentucky Catholic* where her column, "Pray About It," spanned a decade.

Kristi Hemingway loves her life in Denver, Colorado, where she works as a teacher, writer, and actress. Her perfect day includes gardening, biking, French food, dancing, and snuggling with her husband and two children. She has recently completed a snarky spiritual memoir and her first novel. E-mail her at klhemingway@comcast.net.

Warren F. Holland received his Bachelor of Arts from Washington & Lee University in 1990 and his Master of International Business Studies from the University of South Carolina in 1993. He is currently employed by Bank of America Merrill Lynch and lives in Charlotte, North Carolina, with his wife and three children.

Dawn Holt received a Bachelor of Science degree, a Master of Education degree, and a Ph.D. in Educational Leadership. She is currently a counselor at Fuller Performance Learning Center in Fayetteville, North Carolina. This is her third contribution to *Chicken Soup for the Soul*. Please e-mail her at dawnholt@yahoo.com.

Kathleen Rice Kardon retired from teaching English to middle school students in 2009. She is a local playwright, actor, and part of a writers' group that meets monthly to write poetry, fiction, and non-fiction. Kathi loves spending time with her children, grandchildren, and her bulldog, Angus. She can be reached at kathkard@satx.rr.com.

Heidi Krumenauer has published more than 1,200 newspaper and magazine articles, has authored nine books, and has contributed to more than a dozen book projects. Her professional career, though, is in upper management with an insurance company. Heidi and her husband raise their two sons in Southern Wisconsin.

Jeremy Langford is an award-winning author whose books include *Seeds of Faith* and *The Spirit of Notre Dame*. He is the Communications Director for the Chicago Province of the Jesuits and runs the Langford Literary Agency. He lives in Evanston, Illinois, with his wife and their three children. E-mail: jereditor@aol.com.

Marianne LaValle-Vincent is the Executive Director of an adult home in Auburn, New York. She has published three full-length poetry collections and hundreds of short stories. She resides in Syracuse, New York, with her daughter Jess and her extended family, which includes three grandchildren.

Janeen Lewis is a freelance writer living in central Kentucky with her husband and two children. She has previously been published in several newspapers, magazines, and three *Chicken Soup for the Soul* anthologies. Please e-mail her at jlewis0402@netzero.net.

Jaye Lewis is an award-winning inspirational writer who sees life from a unique perspective, celebrating the miracles in the everyday. Jaye enjoys being a part of the Chicken Soup for the Soul family. She lives and writes in the mountains of Virginia. Visit Jaye's website at www.entertainingangels.org.

Sandra Life is devoted to her remaining five children (and their spouses), one to whom she gave birth and four from Korea whom she and Richard adopted. Today the "lights of her life" are ten grandchildren, including one adopted. Sandra remains an active volunteer in church and community.

Linda Mainard has lived in Milwaukie, Oregon, for thirty-three years. Linda and her husband have four children and have three grandchildren. She has had an amazing life. There is nothing that she cares about more then her family and her faith. This story is a record of that love.

Debra Manford is a fifty-five-year-old woman with three grown children and many grandchildren. She is currently working full-time with mentally challenged adults. Debra loves her job, loves her life, and truly believes the best is yet to come! Contact her via e-mail at free_2bee@hotmail.com.

Tina Wagner Mattern is a Portland, Oregon, writer who has been blessed with every kind of miracle possible and is ever so grateful. This will be the third story published in *Chicken Soup for the Soul.* Contact her via e-mail at freddiestina@gmail.com.

Kathy McGovern holds Masters degrees in both Liturgical Studies and Sacred Scripture. She has published numerous articles on Scripture and spirituality and is the composer of the popular Christmas song "Mary Had a Baby." She and her husband Ben Lager live in Denver, Colorado. Reach her at mcgovern.kathy@yahoo.com.

Kimberly McLagan is a wife, mother of four, writer, and Christian speaker with a compelling testimony of how to survive the trenches of infertility. A former corporate executive, consultant, and college instructor of management and marketing, her new book supports women experiencing barrenness with prayers and direction. www. infertilityprayerresource.com.

Terri Ann Meehan grew up in Ohio where most of her stories take place. Since moving to England in 1991, Terri enjoys writing about family, friends, and the memories they shared. She has been published in several books and magazines, including various *Chicken Soup for the Soul* titles.

Marie-Therese Miller lives in New York with her husband and five children. She is the author of *Distinguished Dogs, Helping Dogs, Hunting and Herding Dogs, Police Dogs*, and *Search and Rescue Dogs* (Chelsea House, 2007). Her stories appeared in *Chicken Soup for the Preteen Soul 2* and *Chicken Soup for the Soul: Love Stories*. Contact her via e-mail at thisisthelife@hvc.rr.com.

Martha Moore taught English for many years. She is an award-winning author of three young adult and middle-grade novels: *Under the Mermaid Angel, Angels on the Roof*, and *Matchit*. She believes that childhood experiences are important. Some are miracles in themselves. Others become miracles when we share them.

Pat Tiernan Morris is married with three children. The story "Mustard Seed Angel" is a message of faith inspired by her late daughter Tera and friends they met along the journey. www.mycmsite.com/ patmorris. Lisa Dolensky, the author of the story, is a mom to three miracles, pre-K teacher, and ghostwriter who has a site at www. wingblots.com.

Lava Mueller lives in Vermont. She enjoys hiking with her daughter, playing games with her son, and going on dates to really good restaurants with her husband. Lava wakes each morning at 3:00 a.m. to meditate and give thanks for the amazing grace that fills her life. She can be reached via e-mail at lavamueller@yahoo.com.

Brittany Newell, an avid opera singer, has recently written her first novel. Previous short stories/essays have been published in *Chicken Soup for the Soul, Dylan Times*, and *The Ark Newspaper*. In 2008 her play received an honorable mention in Young Playwrights Festival National Playwriting Competition. Brittany, 16, is a junior in high school.

Herchel E. Newman, has been writing seriously for ten years, but has been a seasoned storyteller all his adult life. He is a skilled photographer, enjoys motorcycle riding with his club, and as a family man, he and his wife enjoy mentoring young married couples. Please e-mail him at ZoomN500@juno.com.

Sherry O'Boyle is a writer living in Eugene, Oregon, and has been published in several magazines, including *Oregon Coast, Northwest Travel, E/The Environmental Magazine*, and the *Catholic Sentinel*. In 2008, she received her Master's degree in Adult & Higher Education Leadership from Oregon State University. Sherry enjoys camping, fishing, traveling, and visiting with family.

Romona Olton received her Bachelor of Science in Chemistry, with honors, and Master of Philosophy in Chemistry from the University of the West Indies St. Augustine in 2005. She teaches science at a secondary school in West Trinidad. Romona enjoys kayaking, hiking, and working with children. Please e-mail her at: romona_olton@hotmail.com.

Sharon Patterson, retired educator, career military wife, and leader in women's ministry, has written works of inspirational encouragement for over thirty years. Sharon's most recent publications are two books, *A Soldier's Strength from the Psalms* and *Healing for the Holes in Our Souls*.

Donna Paulson lives on the island of Martha's Vineyard with her four children, dog, and cat. She works at a local Counsel on Aging and enjoys writing, reading a good novel, going to church, laughing with friends and family, and looking for sea glass. You can e-mail her at dpaulson31@verizon.net.

Gisele Reis instilled in her children a belief in the miraculous and the joy of life. She grew up in Belgium during WWII, where she served in the Resistance along with her siblings and parents. Gisele allowed Marie-Therese Miller to write about Mariette's miraculous cure in hopes that it would inspire others. Please visit Marie-Therese Miller's website: www.marie-theresemiller.com.

Kelly Stewart Rich received her Bachelor of Science in Education and Master of Science in Education from the College of the Southwest. She is a lifelong resident of Hobbs, New Mexico, where she and her husband raise their four children. Kelly can be reached via e-mail at krich@valornet.com.

Christina Robertson received her Bachelor of Science with honors from Bethel College in 2000 and her Masters Degree in Education from Cumberland University in 2006. She teaches seventh and eighth grades in Middle Tennessee. Christina enjoys reading, singing, drama, and working with children. She hopes to become a published author in the near future.

Meet Our Contributors!

Courtney Rusk received her BA, with honors, and master of adult education from Northwestern State University. She teaches twelfth grade English in Pineville, Louisiana, where she lives with her husband and two children. Courtney has a passion for reading, teaching, and spending time with her family. Please e-mail her at courtleerusk@yahoo.com.

David Michael Smith believes in miracles, including three special ones: his wife, Geri, and two children, Rebekah and Matthew. He's a Marketing Specialist for the DE Department of Agriculture by day and writer by night. He's been widely published in the past, including in *Chicken Soup for the Soul*. Please e-mail David at davidandgeri@hotmail.com.

Jeffrey Brooks Smith is a comedian/writer/speaker who is proud to be Catholic. He works to spread that pride to everyone he meets. He performs his humor-based apologetics programs to Catholic groups around the country. He can be reached via e-mail at Jeffrey.smoth@kofc.org.

Mary Z. Smith resides in Richmond, Virginia, with her husband, Barry, of thirty-three years. They enjoy visits from their grown children and grandchildren. When Mary isn't writing for her favorite publications like *Chicken Soup for the Soul*, *Guideposts*, and *Angels on Earth*, she can be found walking her Rat Terrier Frankie or gardening.

Marisa A. Snyder earned her BS in 1992. She taught in several capacities and coordinated religious programs. She is blessed with two sons and a fiancé. Marisa has Stargardt's disease, prompting her boutique which features "Seeing with Style" necklaces. She writes poetry, inspirational stories, and tween novels. Contact her at marisasboutique@yahoo.com.

Everyday Catholicism

Johnna Stein is happily married and the mother to two spunky teenagers. She loves teaching reading to dyslexic kids. She's an avid reader and writer, and her stories have appeared in *Chicken Soup for the Soul, Guide, Susie Magazine,* and *Discipleship Journal.* Her first middle-grade humorous novel is nearly ready to find a home.

Dawn J. Storey is a mother, writer, and systems analyst for a major corporation. Although technical writing is her focus on the job, she enjoys writing inspirational stories with the hopes of uplifting readers. Dawn's writing reflects the feeling side of life.

Joyce Sudbeck received her Associate's Degree, with honors, in 1986. She recently left her Marketing Department position at Liguori Publications to pursue new challenges. Joyce enjoys choir, composing, piano, poetry, crocheting, knitting, sewing, cooking, and writing. Joyce plans to continue writing poetry, short stories, and perhaps a novel.

Donna Teti has been published in both *Guideposts* magazine and Cecil Murphey's *Christmas Miracles.* She is also a 2008 winner of the Guideposts Writers Workshop Contest. Through her inspirational writings, Donna hopes to bring comfort to those who are grieving. Her website is donnateti.com and her e-mail is donnateti@verizon.net.

Terrie Todd writes from Portage la Prairie, Manitoba, Canada, where she is an administrative assistant at City Hall. She and her husband Jon are the parents of three adult children and have two adorable grandsons. You can reach her via e-mail at jltodd@mts.net.

Kristen Torres-Toro received her BA in English in 2007 from Toccoa Falls College and woke up three weeks later in the Amazon jungle. She is a missionary with Adventures In Missions and hopes to one day publish a novel. Please e-mail her at kristentorrestoro@gmail.com.

Christine M. Trollinger is a freelance writer whose stories have been published in several anthologies and magazines. She is a widow, mother of three, and enjoys working with the local animal rescue groups. Please e-mail her at trollys_2@yahoo.com.

Connie Vagg is a California native, retired secretary, has two daughters, and granny to four. Her annual Christmas tradition is making personalized gingerbread houses, and she is fondly referred to by family and friends as "The Gingerbread Lady." Connie's first story was published in *Chicken Soup for the Soul: Living Catholic Faith.* Contact her at cvagg@netzero.net.

Beverly F. Walker lives in Greenbrier, Tennessee, with her retired husband. She enjoys writing, photography, and scrapbooking pictures of her grandchildren. She has stories in many *Chicken Soup for the Soul* books, and in *Angel Cats: Divine Messengers of Comfort.*

Meet LeAnn Thieman

LeAnn Thieman is a nationally acclaimed professional speaker, author, and nurse who was "accidentally" caught up in the Vietnam Orphan Airlift in 1975. Her book, *This Must Be My Brother*, details her daring adventure of helping to rescue 300 babies as Saigon was falling to the Communists. LeAnn and her incredible story have been featured in *Newsweek Magazine's Voices of the Century* issue, FOX News, CNN, PBS, BBC, PAX-TV's *It's A Miracle*, and countless radio and TV programs.

Today, as a renowned motivational speaker, LeAnn inspires audiences to balance their lives, truly live their priorities, and make a difference in the world.

After her story was featured in *Chicken Soup for the Mother's Soul*, LeAnn became one of Chicken Soup for the Soul's most prolific writers. That, and her devotion to thirty years of nursing, made her the ideal co-author of *Chicken Soup for the Nurse's Soul*. She went on to co-author *Chicken Soup for the Caregiver's Soul*; *Chicken Soup for the Father and Daughter Soul*; *Chicken Soup for the Mother and Son Soul*; *Chicken Soup for the Grandma's Soul*; *Chicken Soup for the Christian Woman's Soul*; *Chicken Soup for the Christian Soul 2*; *Chicken Soup for the Adopted Soul*; *Chicken Soup for the Nurse's Soul, Second Dose*; *Chicken Soup for the Soul, Inspiration for Nurses*; *Chicken Soup for the Soul, A Book of Miracles*; and *Chicken Soup for the Soul,*

Answered Prayers. Her life-long practice of her Catholic faith led her to co-author *Chicken Soup for the Soul: Living Catholic Faith.*

LeAnn is one of about ten percent of speakers worldwide to have earned the Certified Speaking Professional Designation award and in 2008 she was inducted into the Speakers Hall of Fame.

She and Mark, her husband of fifty years, reside in Colorado.

For more information about LeAnn's books and programs, or to schedule her for a presentation, please contact her at:

LeAnn Thieman, CSP, CPAE
6600 Thompson Drive
Fort Collins, CO 80526
1-970-223-1574
www.LeAnnThieman.com
e-mail LeAnn@LeAnnThieman.com

Sophia Institute

Sophia Institute is a nonprofit institution that seeks to nurture the spiritual, moral, and cultural life of souls and to spread the Gospel of Christ in conformity with the authentic teachings of the Roman Catholic Church.

Sophia Institute Press fulfills this mission by offering translations, reprints, and new publications that afford readers a rich source of the enduring wisdom of mankind.

Sophia Institute also operates the popular online resource CatholicExchange.com. *Catholic Exchange* provides world news from a Catholic perspective as well as daily devotionals and articles that will help readers to grow in holiness and live a life consistent with the teachings of the Church.

In 2013, Sophia Institute launched Sophia Institute for Teachers to renew and rebuild Catholic culture through service to Catholic education. With the goal of nurturing the spiritual, moral, and cultural life of souls, and an abiding respect for the role and work of teachers, we strive to provide materials and programs that are at once enlightening to the mind and ennobling to the heart; faithful and complete, as well as useful and practical.

Sophia Institute gratefully recognizes the Solidarity Association for preserving and encouraging the growth of our apostolate over the course of many years. Without their generous and timely support, this book would not be in your hands.

www.SophiaInstitute.com
www.CatholicExchange.com
www.SophiaInstituteforTeachers.org

Sophia Institute Press® is a registered trademark of Sophia Institute. Sophia Institute is a tax-exempt institution as defined by the Internal Revenue Code, Section 501(c)(3). Tax ID 22-2548708.